T0328794

Cambridge Elements ≡

Elements in the Politics of Development
edited by
Rachel Beatty Riedl
Einaudi Center for International Studies and Cornell University
Ben Ross Schneider
Massachusetts Institute of Technology

Mario Einaudi
CENTER FOR
INTERNATIONAL STUDIES

 MIT CENTER FOR INTERNATIONAL STUDIES

GREED AND GUNS

Imperial Origins of the Developing World

Atul Kohli
Princeton University

CAMBRIDGE
UNIVERSITY PRESS

Shaftesbury Road, Cambridge CB2 8EA, United Kingdom

One Liberty Plaza, 20th Floor, New York, NY 10006, USA

477 Williamstown Road, Port Melbourne, VIC 3207, Australia

314–321, 3rd Floor, Plot 3, Splendor Forum, Jasola District Centre, New Delhi – 110025, India

103 Penang Road, #05–06/07, Visioncrest Commercial, Singapore 238467

Cambridge University Press is part of Cambridge University Press & Assessment, a department of the University of Cambridge.

We share the University's mission to contribute to society through the pursuit of education, learning and research at the highest international levels of excellence.

www.cambridge.org

Information on this title: www.cambridge.org/9781009199742

DOI: 10.1017/9781009199759

First published 2022

A catalogue record for this publication is available from the British Library.

ISBN 978-1-009-19974-2 Paperback
ISSN 2515-1584 (online)
ISSN 2515-1576 (print)

Greed and Guns

Imperial Origins of the Developing World

Elements in the Politics of Development

DOI: 10.1017/9781009199759
First published online: October 2022

Atul Kohli
Princeton University
Author for correspondence: Atul Kohli, kohli@princeton.edu

Abstract: This Element studies the causes and the consequences of modern imperialism. The focus is on British and US imperialism in the nineteenth and twentieth centuries, respectively. The dynamics of both formal and informal empires are analyzed. The argument is that imperialism is moved mainly by the desire of major powers to enhance their national economic prosperity. They do so by undermining sovereignty in peripheral countries and establishing open economic access. The impact on the countries of the periphery tends to be negative. In a world of states, then, national sovereignty is an economic asset. Since imperialism seeks to limit the exercise of sovereign power by subject people, there tends to be an inverse relationship between imperialism and development: The less control a state has over its own affairs, the less likely it is that the people of that state will experience economic progress.

Keywords: imperialism, developing countries, colonialism, informal empire, underdevelopment

ISBNs: 9781009199742 (PB), 9781009199759 (OC)
ISSNs: 2515-1584 (online), 2515-1576 (print)

Contents

1 Introduction

Global forces have shaped the politics and economics of the developing world, at times decisively. First there was European colonialism in Asia, Africa, and Latin America. Alongside, there were a variety of less formal external influences without territorial control, such as Britain's informal empire in nineteenth-century Latin America, China, and the Middle East. Non-Western powers like Japan also created their own regional empire in the early twentieth century. Following World War II, the influence of the USA on the developing world grew markedly. Notwithstanding some early forays into colonialism – such as in the Philippines – the USA in the second half of the twentieth century eschewed formal empire; the American way to empire instead was informal, including military interventions, fostering coups, supporting pro-American regimes in select client states, and pressuring developing countries to open their markets to American goods, investment, and finance. At present, the USA maintains nearly 800 military bases in seventy countries across the world.

Why do metropolitan powers repeatedly expand into peripheral countries? What is the impact of such expansions? In this Element, I provide an overview of how modern imperialism has shaped the developing world. The causes, strategies, and the consequences of imperialism are analyzed. The focus is on the British Empire in the nineteenth century and American efforts to shape the global periphery in the twentieth century, with a nod to Japanese imperialism in the first half of the twentieth century.[1] Both formal and informal empire are discussed. I argue that what drives modern imperialism is the desire of metropolitan powers to enhance their national economic prosperity, an outcome that is both a desired end in itself and a means to enhanced power; the drive for imperialism is thus both economic and political. In order to force open economic access, imperialist powers pursue their overseas interests by undermining sovereignty in peripheral countries. Whereas formal political control in colonies readily facilitates economic opening, stable-but-subservient regimes in peripheral countries also enable metropolitan powers to penetrate their economies. Forced economic access, in turn, enables metropolitan countries to take advantage of peripheral economies via mechanisms that vary anywhere from naked plunder to more sophisticated design of trade, investment, and financial transactions. The impact of imperialism on peripheral countries thus tends to be negative, even sharply negative, especially when assessed from the standpoint of economic well-being.

---

[1] Other European empires, such as that of the French, are mentioned in passing but not discussed in any detail.

The central argument of this Element is that, in a world of states, national sovereignty is an economic asset. Although national sovereignty may not be sufficient to put a developing country on a path of progress, it is often a necessary precondition. Since imperialism seeks to limit the exercise of sovereign power by subject people, there tends to be an inverse relationship between imperialism and development: The less control a state has over its own affairs, the less likely it is that people of that state will experience steady, inclusive economic progress.

This argument is based on an extensive investigation of historical and contemporary cases of imperialism in the developing world. These include: British colonialism in India and Nigeria; Britain's informal empire in Argentina, Brazil, Egypt, and China; Japanese colonialism in Korea; the early twentieth-century expansion of the USA into Cuba, the Philippines, and China; American interventions during the Cold War in Korea, Iran, Vietnam, and Chile; and more recent efforts by the USA to impose the Washington Consensus on Latin America and to intervene militarily in Iraq. Given the scope of this Element, I do not provide historical details; my interpretation of these cases is readily available elsewhere (mainly Kohli, 2020, but also, Kohli, 2004). Evidence from these cases will be used instead in this slim Element as illustrations in support of general arguments about the causes, strategies, and the impact of imperialism, both formal and informal.

1.1 Clearing the Brush

It may be useful to set aside three sets of issues at the outset, one definitional, one historical, and one theoretical. *First*, it is important to acknowledge that imperialism is a controversial term. The term imperialism in this study directs attention to efforts of one state to exert control over another state or people. Few observers are likely to take exception to the use of the term imperialism when control of one state over another includes direct territorial control, as in formal colonies. Colonialism, however, is a subset, albeit an important subset, of imperialism. In modern times, another major subset of imperialism is informal empire. These are situations in which a metropolitan power exercises significant influence over a peripheral country, but without controlling its territory or government. Since the issues of how much influence is "significant," and how metropolitan countries exercise such influence, involve matters of judgment, the use of the term informal empire tends to be more controversial. As used in this study, an informal empire is defined with reference to three conditions: imperial powers exercise veto power over key policies in client states; under normal circumstances, the ruling elite in the metropole and the periphery collaborate; and when such relations of domination and subordination are challenged, imperial powers use (or threaten to use) coercion to seek compliance. The use of coercion is especially important for judging a relationship as imperial because it helps distinguish informal empire from more commonplace inequality of power or situations of economic dependence across states, as well as from hegemonic relations that involve some degree of willing collaboration between a superior and a weaker power.

Second, any student of modern imperialism needs to keep in mind a simple but important historical point: Empires and imperialism are age-old phenomena. There is much to be learned from studying land-based and other forms of precapitalist empires (Eisenstadt, 1993; Burbank and Cooper, 2010). In this study, however, I focus mainly on the dynamics of overseas empires in the age of industrial capitalism, say, from the second half of the eighteenth century onwards. This is because imperialism in the capitalist era took a distinctive turn and is worthy of study in its own right. Capitalist empires were a product of modern economic growth that was characterized by growing productivity. The needs of economic growth propelled industrializing powers to search for new markets and for cheaper raw materials, a search that eventually led to the division of the world into an industrial core and a commodity-producing periphery. Over time, this division into core and periphery came to be associated with sharp disparities in the standards of living across the Global North and South. Such disparities were rare in precapitalist empires. For example, the per capita income of peninsular Italy – the heart of the Roman Empire – in 14 AD was less than double the average per capita income of the rest of the empire (Madison, 2007, 52). The same held true for most traditional land empires, as well as for modern-day land empires, such as that run by the former Soviet Union. By contrast, the emergence of industrial capitalism, first in Western Europe, and then in the USA and Japan, was accompanied by a growing divergence in standards of living across the core and periphery. Again, for example, the per capital income of England around 1600 was less than double that of China and India; by 1950, however, England was ten times wealthier than the two Asian giants (Madison, 2007, table A.7, 382). The dynamism of industrial capitalism in core countries propelled imperial expansion into peripheral parts of the world and imperialism, in turn, reinforced the division of the world into a wealthier core and a poor periphery. The underlying dynamics of imperialism in the age of capitalism is thus the main focus of this Element.

Third, readers with scholarly inclinations may be interested in knowing at the outset how the argument about causes and consequences of imperialism presented here differs or overlaps with other existing accounts. The study of causes and consequences of imperialism is often compartmentalized. Diplomatic historians and scholars of international relations generally pursue the issue of why imperialists imperialize. The issue of how imperialism shaped the global periphery is just as often debated by a distinct set of scholars of political economy of development. In this Element, I try to systematically connect these two strands of scholarly concerns and hope to move them in new directions.

More specifically, my explanation about the causes of imperialism is in dialogue with liberal, realist, and Marxist standpoints on imperialism. The details will emerge in due course. Suffice it to note at the outset that, for the most part, I disagree with those liberal interpretations of imperialism that suggest that imperialism in the modern age is foolish, "atavistic," or a mistake (Schumpeter, 1951).[2] I argue instead that the evidence supports the view that metropolitan powers repeatedly pursue imperialism so as to seek economic and political advantage in far-flung, underdeveloped regions of the world. Metropolitan powers do not always succeed in achieving what they set out to achieve, but that is a different issue than why they pursue imperialism in the first place.

As to the well-debated issue of economic versus political motivations behind imperialism, I will take exceptions to some of the more standard but narrower arguments. For example, I will again show that evidence does not support the view that what moves imperialism are concerns of national security (Cohen, 1973). Oh, at times security concerns are important; how could they not be in matters of foreign actions of nations, especially when rivalries among major powers are the focus? For the most part, however, when imperialism was pursued by hegemonic nations, such as Britain in the nineteenth century, and the USA in the second half of the twentieth century, their national security was hardly threatened, certainly not by (or in) peripheral countries. Similarly, the purely economic arguments, such as that of Hobson (1902), also fall short. It is not that economic motivation is not central to imperialism – it is – but imperialism is a state-led phenomenon. Economic needs of metropolitan powers are often defined by their respective governments. And government leaders represent more than just the interests of the economic elite of the metropolitan countries. Instead, I will argue that states in the modern world constantly worry about the prosperity of their national societies. As such, they look for policies that might enhance wealth, especially of their elites, but also of their citizens. For rulers of great powers, the world becomes an oyster. Seeking economic opportunities

---

[2] Another strand in liberal thinking is that imperialism is about doing "good" – anywhere from saving souls to bringing democracy. I will eventually suggest that there is very little in the historical evidence to support such views, though plenty of such rhetoric exists in the historical record that helped legitimize imperial ventures. For a more detailed bibliography, see Kohli (2020).

beyond national borders thus periodically emerges as a viable option for great powers. When peripheral countries resist such advances, metropolitan powers use force to undermine sovereign control and to pry open peripheral economies; the pursuit of profits with force – *Greed and Guns* – is then the core dynamics of imperialism.

My argument on the impact of imperialism in turn connects with both dependency and proglobalization standpoints on the developing world, making a case instead for state-led capitalist development. The suggestion that imperialism impacted peripheral countries negatively is hardly novel. It has been made by many nationalist and left-leaning critics of imperialism; it was also a central claim of the dependency literature (Palma, 1978). I broadly agree with this line of thinking but posit different underlying mechanisms. Instead of arguing à la Wallerstein (1974) that development and underdevelopment are a systematic product of the "capitalist world system," I focus on the role of sovereign states in both propelling development and imperialism on the one hand and, on the other hand, on the loss of sovereignty and the related absence of national autonomy in the periphery as a source of underdevelopment. This focus on the importance of sovereignty and state intervention then also puts me at odds with those who champion open globalization in the contemporary era as the road to prosperity (Bhagwati, 2004). I suggest instead that success at late development requires a more selective embrace of the global economy, mediated by sovereign and effective states. The success of Japan in the nineteenth century, and of China and India at the turn of the twenty-first century, exemplify this proposition.

1.2 Organization of the Element

The main issues that I analyze in this Element are: why imperialists imperialize; strategies of imperialism; and the impact of imperialism. The next three core sections take up each of these themes in turn. As readers make their way through these brief sections, it will be important to keep in mind that, in my account, the issues of causes, strategies, and the consequences of imperialism are systematically interlinked: In order to understand the negative consequences of imperialism on the developing world (Section 4), one first needs to understand how imperialists undermined sovereignty in the peripheral regions of the world (Section 3), but the need to undermine sovereignty makes sense only if one comprehends at the outset that what metropolitan powers were trying to achieve was to gain economic advantage over peripheral countries by prying open their respective economies (Section 2). In the concluding section (Section 5), I will reiterate the central themes, raise some normative issues, and speculate about near future trends, especially emerging Chinese imperialism.

2 Why Imperialists Imperialize

In the age of capitalism, metropolitan states pursue imperialism as a strategy to enhance national economic prosperity. This is the main proposition that the historical evidence reviewed in this section supports. The reasoning behind this proposition is fairly straightforward. All modern states pursue economic prosperity. They do so for a variety of reasons, but mainly because in a world of growing economies – a modern phenomenon itself – states cannot afford to sit still. Maintaining relative national prosperity is an essential component of relative national power in the modern world and thus of preserving national security. National security of any state rests on a strong economic base. Hence, states seek to promote national prosperity. For powerful capitalist states, this urge inclines them to ensure economic opportunities for their capitalists at home and abroad. Beyond national borders, this implies helping national firms find markets and investment opportunities overseas, as well as to manage external finances. The most powerful capitalist states thus seek to create an open global economy – or at least economic openness in countries that they dominate – in which their competitive firms can outsell or produce goods for others. When lesser powers resist, imperialism is likely to follow; forced economic opening is an integral aspect of modern imperialism. What imperialists seek to tame then is sovereign and effective state power on the global periphery.

In the historical discussion that follows, I will provide evidence to suggest that both British and American imperialism follow this logic; that both are best understood as processes of establishing global dominance aimed at creating open-economy imperium. As we review historical materials, there will be occasions to examine this proposition against such other cases as that of Japanese regional imperialism, as well as to qualify this core proposition. At times, both Britain and the USA pursued imperial actions that were aimed more narrowly at balance-of-power considerations rather than the broader goal of national economic prosperity. And in yet other instances, imperial intervention was on behalf of narrow capitalist interests rather than that of the nation as a whole. Some qualifications notwithstanding, much of the evidence supports the suggestion that British and American decision-makers imperialized peripheral countries with the hope of enriching their mother countries.

2.1 British Imperialism

The British came late to imperialism.[3] By the time that the East India Company started exploring trading opportunities in the early sixteenth century in India

---

[3] Major works on the British Empire include Hyam (1976); Cain and Hopkins (2002); and Darwin (2009). The five volumes of *The Oxford History of the British Empire* (editor, Wm. Roger Louis,

and elsewhere, the Spaniards and the Portuguese had already established colonies in various parts of the world, especially in the New World. The Dutch East India Company was also ahead in the fray for overseas riches; they pioneered the idea of armed trade organized by a joint stock company that the East India Company eventually emulated and surpassed. A variety of private merchants in England had requested royal support for overseas trading in the sixteenth century, mostly in vain. The Tudors of England were too busy at the time with such other pressing matters as centralizing the power of the monarchy, creating a greater Britain, and the Reformation. Only late in her reign did Queen Elizabeth start granting royal charters to overseas traders that gave private companies monopoly trading rights in one part of the world or another. Trading companies were obviously looking for profitable trade overseas, and the English Crown, in turn, strapped as it was for resources, hoped to tax such trading profits to support the national exchequer. England's overseas expansion thus began with private actors – armed with royal charters – leading voyages as disparate as those that brought settlers to the Chesapeake Bay, moved fortune seekers to grab islands from the Spaniards in the Caribbean, and sought profits in luxury products in the East, especially in India.

Over the next three centuries, the British Empire grew to be the most important of Europe's overseas empires. Following the loss of its American colony, India became the most important of Britain's formal colonies. So, if one is trying to understand British imperialism in the Global South, understanding British motives in India is a good place to begin. During the nineteenth century, moreover, the British supplemented their colonial holdings by establishing informal influence over Latin America, the Middle East, and China. Motives that drove the British to expand into these regions then further help us understand what drove the British imperial project during the Victorian era. And finally, of course, there was the scramble for Africa toward the end of the nineteenth century; this too needs to be understood. In the discussion that follows, Nigeria provides a specific example of British interests in West Africa.

Britain ruled India for nearly two centuries, with the state-supported East India Company at the helm during the first century (1757–1857), and as a direct Crown colony during the second (1857–1947). While British motives in India changed over time – two centuries is a long time – economic considerations were nearly always at the forefront. The East India Company came to India as traders, hoping to make profits, and profits they did make. While the Mughal rule in India was intact during the seventeenth and early eighteenth centuries,

---

published in various years) also provide an uneven collection of essays on specialized topics. Hobsbawm (1989) is also deeply informative.

much of the trade between India and Britain was on commercial terms: Company ships from England brought bullion – the price of which was much cheaper in Europe due to the looting of the Aztecs and the Incas by the Spaniards – and exchanged it for Indian textiles, the demand for which was growing in England. The British state both supported the East India Company and taxed its profits; both gained from this overseas trade.

As the Mughal rule started disintegrating in India in the early eighteenth century, and as Britain consolidated and expanded state power during the same period, commercial trade between Britain and India became more and more politicized. The state-supported East India Company increasingly used force to alter the terms of trade with India in its own favor; for example, the Company increasingly refused to pay custom duty to local rulers, thus depriving them of taxes while enhancing their own profitability. Protectionist legislation passed in early 1700 also kept Indian textiles out of Britain; Indian textiles bought by the East India Company were now sold to other European markets, and facilitated the slave trade, while British textile manufacturing started to come into its own behind protectionist walls. By the middle of the century, of course, the East India Company started acquiring territory in India, starting with Bengal in 1757. From then on, Company rule expanded over India following a discernable pattern: The Company taxed conquered territories – especially its agricultural production – at a high level, channeled these revenues to further build and arm a British Indian army, and then used this army to conquer yet more Indian territory. Extraction thus led to more extraction. By the early nineteenth century, the East India Company had established rule over much of modern-day India, Pakistan, and Bangladesh.

The revenues that the East India Company extracted from India in the late eighteenth and the early nineteenth centuries averaged some 18 percent of the gross domestic product (GDP) of the Indian territories controlled by the Company. Nearly 60 percent of these revenues came from taxing India's poor peasantry. The most important benefit for Britain from its Indian colony in the eighteenth and the nineteenth centuries was that nearly half of the Indian revenues were used to build and maintain a massive British Indian army. This army was not only used to conquer and control India, but, over time, it became central to Britain's imperial expansion in Asia, Africa, and the Middle East, including the Opium Wars in China. The beauty of it from the British point of view was this: The British Indian army enabled Britain to expand its global power substantially, without paying a penny for it. Indian revenues, as we will see, also enabled Britain to expand trade and thus helped with its balance of payments; this was important because warring Britain, especially in the early nineteenth century (e.g. Napoleonic Wars), was often strapped for foreign exchange, a gap that could not have been filled without foreign exchange inflows from such colonies as Ireland and India.

As to private benefits, the Company of course came to India primarily to make profits. With access to Indian revenues, the mechanisms via which the Company made profits modified. Instead of bringing bullion on ships from England to procure products in India – which were then sold in England and elsewhere – now the Company simply used Indian revenues to buy calicos, chintz, spices, and indigo in India for sale back in Europe. The Company also charged its expenses – including for buildings and ships in London, and personnel salaries the world over – to its Indian revenues. And finally, the Company started using Indian revenues to promote the growing and processing of opium in India; this opium in turn found a market in China, where it was exchanged both for silver and, increasingly, for tea, for which demand in England and elsewhere (including the USA) was growing. Indian revenues thus facilitated huge profits for the Company and its shareholders, many of whom were increasingly British parliamentarians.

During the first half of the nineteenth century, Britain and its colonial relations underwent important changes. Britain was increasingly a manufacturing nation, with textiles in the lead. Following the Napoleonic Wars, Britain's global power was also unmatched. The East India Company lost its monopoly to trade with India in 1813. From then on, the Company became mainly a set of state-supported rulers of India, while trade with India shifted into the hands of a variety of merchants. Britain increasingly sold textiles to India, the Company in India organized a highly profitable opium trade with China, and opium in China was exchanged for tea that was sold back in Britain. Forced opening of the Indian economy led to decline in manufacturing in India, especially textile manufacturing, and to an increase in commodity exports, especially opium – more on this in Section 4. The triangular trade that adjoined Britain, India, and China enabled Britain's textile manufacturers to sell their products and a variety of British merchants to partake in a profitable trade with a captured colonial market.

Indian aristocracy revolted against Company rule in India in 1857. The economic and political importance of India to Britain was so great by now that virtually no one in Britain questioned the need to hold on to its Indian colony. The British then unleashed its military might on lightly armed Indians, killing some 800,000, and thus established direct Crown rule over India that lasted till the middle of the twentieth century. With India at its feet, the British modified its ruling strategy in India in a more conservative direction. During the second half of the nineteenth century, the British reorganized the armed forces in India so as to avoid any future "mutinies," rationalized the state structure, and reordered its relations with Indian landowning classes so as to incorporate them in a ruling alliance.

Crown rule in India was autocratic and exploitative. Economic benefits to Britain from its Indian colony flowed from both direct actions of the colonial state and indirectly from private transactions lubricated by favorable state policies. As to the fiscal track, the revenues that the colonial state collected in India increased in the post-1857 period, reaching close to 20 percent of Indian GDP. The mainstay of these revenues (40–50 percent) remained taxes on poor peasants. Other major source of revenues included earnings from a state monopoly on the production of opium (much of which was exported to China) and salt for the Indian market (16 and 12 percent, respectively). Nearly half of these revenues continued to be used to support the giant British Indian army. Since this army was increasingly being used to expand the British Empire in territories near India, the Indian colony clearly subsidized British imperialism. Another third or so of the annual Indian revenues were used by the British for simply running the empire in India, including the payment of high salaries to British colonial employees, building summer residences for these employees high up in the foothills of the Himalayas to escape the sweltering Indian heat, and, of course, constructing infrastructure to facilitate trade, as well as the movement of the armed forces, across India. By contrast, as we will see in Section 4, what the British invested in education, health, or irrigation within India was downright miniscule.

From the mid-nineteenth century onward, the importance of private economic transactions between Britain and India grew. Of course, the colonial state provided the necessary framework to facilitate British gains. For example, trade grew steadily in the post-1857 period; British exports were nearly all manufactured goods, and Indian exports were increasingly all commodities. India's economy, which had been opened with force, continued to absorb an increasing percentage of British textile exports (close to 40 percent of the total of British textile exports toward the end of the century); in spite of growing global competition, this in turn enabled one of Britain's core industries to grow throughout the century. Following the Opium Wars with China (more on this later), opium exports from India to China also grew, facilitating profitable purchase of tea from China for the British and other markets. Given the economic security provided by Crown rule, British private investment in India accelerated. Most notable among these was investment to build railways across India; the colonial state in India guaranteed a rate of return of 5 percent on this investment to British investors. The colonial state also managed India's balance of payments carefully so as to ensure that India had enough foreign exchange available to pay for salaries and pensions of British colonial servants, profit remittance, and interest on the public debt. In brief, Crown rule in India finally turned the Indian colony into a true economic colony that took British manufactured goods in exchange for commodity exports, absorbed British investments, including investments with political guarantees on the rate of return, and helped balance Britain's external finances.

Leaving aside areas of white settlement, India was Britain's most important colony, especially in the nineteenth century. If one is trying to understand what drove British imperialism, understanding British motives in India are thus central. The evidence reviewed, albeit in brief, underlines that economic motives were at the heart of British rule in India. Private merchants came to India looking to make profits, the British state supported them with the hope of sharing the profits, and over time, the British state gained the upper hand, ensuring giant economic gains for both the British state and the British economy, including gains for British industrialists. British gains from India probably peaked around Wold War I. After that, the British Century was over. Indians also sensed this changing global situation and slowly but surely demanded independence. We will visit the issue of the negative impact of Britain on India in the subsequent sections. For now, the important conclusion to note is that the pursuit of national economic prosperity is what drove British imperialism in India.

The British military victory over Napoleon in 1815 confirmed Britain's growing status as the world's paramount power. British statesmen were convinced in the early nineteenth century that sustaining Britain's industrialization and economic dynamism required overseas markets, especially beyond Europe and the USA, and that it was the role of the British state to open such markets. Britain then used its superior power in the post-1815 period to pry open markets in various parts of the world, at times by establishing new colonies, but also by building an informal empire, that is, by creating client states – stable but subservient – without controlling their territory. A brief review of British expansion in Latin America, the Middle East, and China can thus help us further understand the drivers of British imperialism.

Following the disruption caused by the Napoleonic Wars, Spain and Portugal lost control of their American colonies and much of Latin America emerged sovereign. Real sovereignty was short-lived, however, because Britain quickly moved in to establish influence over such significant countries as Argentina, Chile, Brazil, and Mexico. These countries offered fresh economic opportunities for Britain's industrializing economy. British leaders decided rather early that colonizing the continent was neither advisable – the costs of conquest were likely to be very high – nor needed, because the British economy was already competitive. What the British needed in countries like Argentina and Brazil instead were governments that would maintain stability on the one hand, and keep the economy open for British interests on the other hand. Creation of such client states was not always easy; for example, while Brazil was pacified rather quickly, it took more than a decade following independence from Spain for Britain to succeed in establishing a stable-but-subservient government in Argentina. Once client states were established, however, countries like Argentina and Brazil provided lucrative markets for Britain.

For example, during the nineteenth century, Argentina absorbed British manufactured goods and exported commodities produced by a ranching economy. Argentina also absorbed private British investments and loans. There is no denying that the economic elite of Argentina benefitted handsomely from such arrangements; supported by Britain, they put their weight behind governments that would maintain open economic relations with Britain. I will return in due course for a further discussion of how such client states operated, as well as to the impact of such economic interactions on Argentina. For now, the issue at hand is British motives for expanding into a country like Argentina. Britain's primary interest in Latin American countries was economic, and political only in so far as to ensure that stable-but-subservient states pursued pro-British policies. British naval power in the region was pretty well uncontested, at least till much later in the century, with the emergence of the USA as a major power; *real politik* considerations thus played a minimal role in British relations, say, with Argentina. The focus instead was on trade, investments, and loans. Britain's textile exports to Argentina between 1817 and 1874 grew at a staggering 9.4 percent per annum.[4] During the second half of the century, trade continued to grow but included such higher value-added manufactured goods as railway materials. Argentina absorbed enormous amount of British capital, nearly 10 percent of Britain's overall capital outflows between 1865 and 1914 (this was larger than even what was absorbed by India during this period). Ensuring payment on loans owed to British bankers were ongoing issues between Argentina and Britain; over time, however, British interests prevailed, thanks to pressures from the British government. Britain's informal empire in Argentina was thus driven by economic considerations and proved to be of great economic importance for the mother country.

Compared to Argentina, British motives in Egypt were more complex, with both political and economic considerations in play, though economic considerations were often at the forefront. Egypt was of course formally part of the Ottoman Empire in the early part of the nineteenth century, with considerable

---

[4] These data are for volume of exports of cotton goods and for the Southern Cone as a whole. See, Llorca-Jaña (2012), table 2.1, p. 23.

autonomy to manage its own affairs. The Egyptian ruler Muhammed Ali undertook nearly heroic efforts to modernize Egypt in the first half of the nineteenth century: He centralized state power, built a conscription-based army, used state power to expand agricultural production and the exports of long cotton, initiated import-substitution type of industrialization in textiles and armaments, and then used enhanced state power to expand Egyptian influence in the territories nearby, threatening the Ottoman Empire from within. Egyptian success irked Britain, both because it threatened Britain's economic ambitions in the region, and because British plans in the region included maintaining a weak but stable Ottoman Empire. Britain then used its superior power to help the Porte (central government of the Ottoman Empire) suppress Muhammed Ali and, in exchange, imposed a free trade treaty on the Ottoman Empire – the Treaty of Balta Liman in 1838 – including on Egypt. Muhammed Ali's military prowess was thus checked and his efforts to modernize the Egyptian economy were forcibly cut short. With the framework of an informal empire established, Britain established colonial-type economic relations with Egypt. When the Egyptians revolted against their khedives for cooperating with the British, the British ruthlessly crushed such opposition and occupied Egypt in 1882, thus initiating the Scramble for Africa. Thereafter, British influence over Egypt continued well into the twentieth century, at least till 1922, when Egypt gained formal sovereignty, but probably till Nasser's coup in 1952.

While British policy in Egypt during the nineteenth century had to keep an eye on such political considerations as the French and Russian interests in the Ottoman Empire, as well as maintaining steady access to India via Egypt, the British also ensured that Egypt during this period served Britain's economic interests. Following the imposition of a free trade treaty, British exports of textiles and other manufactured goods to Egypt grew significantly, as did Egyptian exports of raw cotton to Britain. The profitable cotton economy of Egypt also attracted British private investment in such related activities as sales, transportation, loans, irrigation, and even land ownership. In addition to integrating Egypt into a colonial economic relationship – I will return to the impact of such relations on Egypt in due course – the other major vector along which Britain gained at the expense of Egypt were huge loans. Egyptian rulers made unwise investments in infrastructure projects and British and French banks lent them large sums of money to do so, often on usurious terms. Loans contracted by the Egyptians to construct the Suez Canal were especially onerous. The British and the French then cooperated to ensure loan repayments; they even demanded and succeeded in running relevant Egyptian economic policies. And in the post-1882 period, the British of course ran the Egyptian government, whose priority it was to ensure that Egypt paid its debts to foreigners. So, yes, *real politik* considerations were more important in British–Egyptian relations in the nineteenth century than, say, in British–Latin American relations, but politically structured trade, investment and financial transactions also brought steady economic gains to Britain during the period.

Finally, in this brief discussion of Britain's informal empire in the nineteenth century, a few comments on Britain's forced opening of China are in order. Britain's interests in China were mostly economic; unlike Egypt, China was the end of the line, not on the way to anywhere. British expansion into China was spearheaded by the East India Company in the late eighteenth century, where the Company used the limited opening of China at Canton to exchange opium produced in India for tea. As already noted, this ingenious triangular trade enabled the British to use land revenues collected in India to produce opium, exchange it for tea in China, and then sell the tea at a good profit back in Britain. From the beginning then, British interest in China was intimately connected to the economic exploitation of its Indian colony. As India started absorbing an increasing amount of British textiles in the early nineteenth century, the need to balance this trade put further pressure on the British to open China more so it could absorb more Indian opium in exchange for more tea for sale back home. Opium imports into China, however, were not only turning an increasingly large number of Chinese into addicts, but purchase of large quantities of opium also required – beyond sale of tea, that is – use of scarce bullion within China. Not surprisingly, Chinese officials sought to limit opium imports into China; these policies of the Qing, in turn, provided the immediate conditions that precipitated the two Opium Wars via which Britain forcibly opened the Chinese economy.

The Opium Wars of the mid-nineteenth century enabled Britain to establish an informal empire over China, a set of arrangements that pretty well lasted up until World War I. Numerous unequal treaties were then imposed on China, creating a thin legal veneer for the exploitation of China. Opium imports from British India to China increased sharply between 1840 and 1870, as did tea exports out of China to Britain. Britain was also now able to export manufactured textiles to China. In addition, Britain made the Chinese pay for the Opium Wars in China by imposing sizable indemnities. China's inability to make these payments readily, in turn, led to growing control over the collection of custom duties in China into British hands. China thus increasingly lost control over the management of its own finances. Over time, China's open economy attracted other Western countries and Japan to take advantage of China. Russia, Germany, and France, for example, carved out their own areas of influence within China. An industrializing Japan eventually attacked China in the 1890s and carved out its own area of influence, but also helped to open up urban spaces for foreign investment. In addition to trade and loans, British private investments in such port cities as Shanghai grew substantially in the post-1895 period. Meanwhile, the Qing state of China came undone, mainly due to internal pressures, but also as a result of imperial machinations. The resulting instability, in turn, opened up opportunities for a variety of Chinese nationalists, including the communists, to recreate a very different China.

If building an informal empire was a prominent trend in British expansionism in the early and the middle of the nineteenth century, territorial annexation again emerged as the main pathway to imperial expansion toward the end of the century. We already noticed this shift in the case of British occupation of Egypt in 1882. The Scramble for Africa then followed the European agreement in Berlin in 1885 to divide up Africa; full colonization of countries like Nigeria then followed. Any full understanding of what drove British imperialism must then also include this last but important late-century burst of expansionism. The motives that drove the British to colonize Nigeria need to be understood both with reference to Britain's longstanding economic interest in West Africa, but also in the context of the broader European Scramble for Africa that gave Nigeria to Britain. Britain had actively participated in the highly profitable slave trade in West Africa for nearly three centuries. After slavery was abolished, British merchants during the nineteenth century bought growing quantities of palm oil from regions that now comprise southern Nigeria and sold such British products as wines and spirits, cotton goods, and some consumer items. Seeking further commercial expansion into West Africa, well before the Scramble, Britain established a coastal colony in Lagos in 1861, something akin to the entrepôt of Hong Kong to China. The British government also supported such private companies as the Royal Niger Company – reminiscent of the East India Company – who not only bought and sold goods in West Africa but performed such political functions as signing treaties with African chiefs that ceded territory, and sending gunboats up and down the Niger into the hinterland. So, yes, Nigeria was eventually formally colonized as a result of the intra-European agreements to divide up Africa, but well before that, Britain pursued commercial interests in the region, and established arrangements to facilitate trade that resembled those of an informal empire.

An informal empire may well have been sufficient for the British to pursue their economic interests in West Africa. However, toward the end of the nineteenth century, the world was changing rapidly and other powers – not only France, but other industrializing powers like the USA, Japan, and Germany, especially Germany – began to compete for colonies across the world. There is no need to deny that such power competition eventually pushed the Europeans to divide up Africa among themselves, and then contributed to Japan annexing Korea and Taiwan on the one hand, and to the USA colonizing the Philippines and establishing a near-colony, or a colony all but in name, in Cuba on the other hand. Before embracing a *real politik* explanation for the Scramble of Africa, however, several important qualifications are in order; political competition for colonies during the period needs to be situated in its economic context.

First, during the second half of the nineteenth century, shipping costs came down and the construction of railways became a global project. These developments increased the potential value of marginal economies on the global periphery, including those of sub-Saharan Africa. For example, with South Africa in mind, feeder railways made the prospect of mining in the interior of Africa a profitable possibility. *Second*, the spread of industrialization to Germany, Japan, and the USA added to the competition for colonial markets, as did the economic turbulence of the late century. And *third*, with reference to West Africa itself, power competition between France and Britain in the region had economic origins. As late industrializers, France often used protectionism at home, as well as in its colonies, to keep British manufactured goods out. The British found this seriously objectionable; this too contributed to their desire to a shift from an informal empire to territorial annexation, as in the case of Nigeria. So, yes, the Scramble for Africa was pushed by growing power competition among European powers, but the substance of that competition was the need to establish political control over potentially valuable economic markets in Africa.

Nigeria was a formal British colony for six decades; it achieved independence in 1960. During this period, British goals in Nigeria were minimal: carry out profitable trade; keep the French out; and ensure that the running of Nigeria did not cost the British exchequer anything. The British thus ran Nigeria – as they did most of their African colonies – on the cheap, expending very little effort either into state building or on modifying the economy. For the most part, the British intervened in those areas that mattered to them – for example, revenue collection, trade promotion, and maintaining minimum political order – and, for the rest, they neglected the colonial Nigerian political economy. We will revisit the issue of the sharply negative consequences of this minimalist colonial strategy for sovereign Nigeria in Section 4. For now, Britain's primary interests in Nigeria are evident in the main colonial policies that the British pursued in Nigeria. The minimal colonial state rested on indirect rule, using traditional strongmen in different regions of Nigeria to collect taxes and to maintain order in their respective domains. Unlike India, the prospects of deriving a large tax base from agriculture in Nigeria were not great; as a result, the British hardly put any energy into creating a civil service that might facilitate revenue collection. Additional tax revenues were derived instead from taxing foreign trade, a political task much easier than taxing incomes directly. A relatively small revenue base in turn facilitated the establishment of a minimal colonial state that helped maintain order and promoted economic transactions between Britain and Nigeria.

Britain's main economic interest in colonial Nigeria was trade. Britain exported textiles, alcohol, building materials, items to build railways, automobiles and bicycles, and other manufactured consumer products. In order to facilitate the growth of such manufactured exports into Nigeria, the colonial state promoted commodity exports from Nigeria back to Britain. These included palm oil, groundnuts, cotton, and cocoa. During the first three decades of colonial rule – before the Great Depression, that is – Britain's trade with Nigeria grew eightfold. Much of this trade was controlled by British companies. The colonial state and British companies thus created what was a fairly classic colonial pattern of exchange of commodities for manufactured goods; private companies were the main beneficiaries, though Britain as a whole also benefitted from the added economic buoyancy. When Nigerian trade eventually recovered following World War II, higher commodity prices during the 1950s benefitted its export economy. Unlike many other colonies, however, foreign investment and financial transactions did not play a large role in British–Nigerian interactions during the six decades of colonial rule. Some foreign investment in consumer goods manufacturing grew in the post–World War II period but the amounts were not large; at independence, only 3 percent of Nigerian GDP originated in manufacturing. British gains from its Nigerian colony – or for that matter, from most of its African colonies, save for Egypt and South Africa – were modest. However, the value of these modest gains has to be judged in relation to the costs of running the colony, which to Britain were negligible.

To sum up, the British Empire in the global periphery sprawled a large part of the globe and unfolded over a couple of centuries. It would be easy to find exceptions to any single explanation for British expansion, whether the explanation be economic, political, or otherwise. However, it would be wise not to succumb to such hopeless conclusions: that it was all "rather complex," that it all "happened haphazardly, without any real patterns," or that a "variety of factors contributed." Based on a review of historical evidence, my suggestion instead is that economic factors were central motivating factors, though, of course, not the only factors. The British state repeatedly sought economic advantages in peripheral economies for its own national economy, including the profitability of its national capitalists, and used superior force to pursue such goals. The use of force for profits thus captures the core dynamics of British imperial expansion – both formal and informal – into areas of the world that we today recognize as the developing world.

2.2 Early American Imperialism

Many Americans believe that, unlike "old" Europe, their country is not an imperial country. This is true in so far as the USA has mostly eschewed formal colonialism. However, like Britain in the nineteenth century, the USA during the long twentieth century has repeatedly sought significant influence without territorial control – or an informal empire – over a variety of poor economies. The USA burst upon the global scene following the Spanish–American War of 1898. Thereafter, the USA established a formal colony in the Philippines, absorbed Hawaii and Puerto Rico, created a near-colony in Cuba, orchestrated regime changes in a number of central American and Caribbean countries, and joined the imperial coalition of Europeans and Japan to keep China stable but subservient. Following World War II, the USA emerged as the most powerful country in the world. During the Cold War then, the USA intervened in numerous developing countries to establish pro-USA governments in power: for example, Iran, Guatemala, Vietnam, Congo, and Chile. And then again, even after the demise of the Soviet Union, US efforts to shape the developing world in its own image hardly decelerated; again, for example, the USA imposed its preferred set of economic policies – the Washington Consensus – on a variety of developing countries, especially those in Latin America, and intervened militarily in countries like Iraq and Afghanistan, again to forcibly install regime change. A brief review of the historical evidence that follows will help us understand the forces that moved the USA to expand into the global periphery; the main suggestion is that, as in the case of Britain, economic considerations often drove American expansionism, though more than in the case of Britain, ideological considerations, especially perceptions and misperceptions of national security also played a role.

During the three decades following the Civil War, state power in the USA became more centralized and the economy industrialized rapidly. Before the Spanish–American War of 1898, the demands for global expansion had also been growing in the USA. With the example of Britain very much on mind, leading Americans argued that the great powers must seek economic opportunities abroad, and to do so, the USA needed a powerful navy.[5] Economic needs added to these arguments. For example, toward the end of the nineteenth century, the argument that the American frontier was closing gained currency. What was needed now, the argument went, was not more land; the USA had already acquired a giant, continent-sized agricultural economy. With the economy industrializing in the post-Civil War period, what was needed were

---

[5] The best book on the period remains LaFeber (1993).

more markets. And these were to be had overseas. The boom-and-bust quality of American end-of-the-century capitalism further contributed to these expansionist arguments. A "glut theory" emerged that suggested that the American economy was producing more than it could consume. Hence, it was suggested, the USA needed overseas markets to smooth out the boom-and-bust cycles of the American economy. With much of the world already colonized, the USA sought access to the few remaining economic spaces. Latin America had long been considered America's "backyard"; with a stronger navy, the Monroe Doctrine now had teeth and a renewed effort to open these southern economies, especially in the Caribbean and Central America, followed. The other giant unoccupied peripheral economy was of course China. The lure of the Chinese market then fed America's overseas imagination.[6] The USA sought the Philippines first and foremost as a stepping stone to China – an American Hong Kong. Following the Spanish–American War then, the USA expanded south of the border, as well as in the distant Pacific, initiating its long century of imperialism.

Ever since the abolition of slavery, American businessmen had invested in plantations and invested in agriculture south of the border. Among the Caribbean countries, Cuba – a Spanish colony – was one of the most significant destinations of American investments.[7] For a few decades preceding the Spanish–American War, however, Cubans had been revolting against Spanish colonialism. Americans were sympathetic to this anticolonial urge, but American economic interests in Cuba were also threatened by Cuban nationalists, especially those who combined appeals to nationalism with calls for social justice, including redistribution of foreign-owned plantation land. While the rhetoric preceding the Spanish–American War in the USA favored Cuban patriots over their Spanish colonizers, official American policy made no commitment to hand Cuba over to Cuban nationalists after the war. American leaders were clear that real sovereignty to Cuba would have adverse impact on American economic interests on the island. However, colonizing or annexing Cuba was also not a viable option; the anticolonial strain in American politics was strong, and there was real reluctance to incorporate a sizable number of blacks to the American body politic. The strategy of how to control Cuba without occupying it then emerged only via trial and error but, in the end, came to resemble what the British had already discovered in the nineteenth century, namely, that establishing an informal empire requires crafting governments in peripheral countries that maintain stability but pursue policies favorable to the metropolitan country.

---

[6] An important book on the subject is McCormick (1967).   [7] See, for example, Healy (1988).

In order to satisfy the antiimperialist strain in American politics, American leaders added an amendment to the legislation that authorized the war against Spain – the Teller Amendment – assuring all and sundry that, following the war, the USA had no interest in occupying or annexing Cuba. With their conscience thus relieved, Americans went to war against Spain and inflicted a rapid and humiliating defeat. Cuba was now American. How to govern it indirectly then came to be codified by the Platt Amendment that pressured the Cubans to accept severe limitations on their sovereignty, including no independent foreign policy, the right of Americans to establish military bases on the island, and to intervene if needed to protect life and property. As a result, Cuba became an American colony in all but name. While some of the Cuban nationalists were bought off, resistance to American influence continued; the US military intervened periodically (e.g. in 1906, 1912, and 1917) to ensure stability and investor profits. Meanwhile, Cuba became a proper economic colony of the USA and remained so till Fidel Castro's revolution in 1959. American trade with Cuba grew sharply following the establishment of political control over Cuba: Cuba exported such commodities as sugar and tobacco to the USA and the USA in turn sold to Cuba a variety of consumer products, mostly manufactured goods. Since commodity exports turned Cuban agriculture profitable, American investments into Cuba also grew. American companies bought up giant pieces of land in Cuba to grow sugarcane and sell sugar back to the USA; over time, US corporations came to own nearly 75 percent of all plantation land in Cuba, with the Rockefeller group and the United Fruit Company among the largest land owners. By the mid-1920s, little Cuba came to be the sixth largest overseas market for US goods and took nearly a quarter of all of American foreign investment.

The other major American colonial acquisition following the Spanish–American War was of course the Philippines. The early motive to acquire the Philippines was that it would serve as an entrepôt to the great market of China. The US military forces in the Pacific sought – and received – the cooperation of Filipino nationalists to oust the Spanish in exchange for some sort of self-determination following the war. The Spaniards were defeated easily but – as in the case of Cuba – the USA did not allow Filipino nationalists to establish a sovereign government over the islands. Unlike Cuba, however, Filipino nationalists were not readily bought off; they chose to fight the USA instead, leading to the mostly forgotten but brutal Philippine–American War that lasted three years. It involved at its peak 70,000 American soldiers, and led to the death of some 20,000 Filipino soldiers and 200,000 Filipino civilians. Following the bloody conquest, the USA chose to govern the Philippines as a colony till the end of World War II.

Having acquired the Philippines, the USA turned it into a proper economic colony. While trappings of democracy were introduced, the Philippines was ruled as a direct American colony. Economic policies pursued by the colonial government encouraged commodity exports from the Philippines in exchange for manufactured imports from the USA. As in the case of Cuba, sugar exports from the Philippines to the USA grew rapidly, more than tenfold between 1903 and 1925. Unlike Cuba, however, American companies were prohibited from buying large tracts of land in the Philippines; this was a result of both the pressures from the sugar lobby in the USA and the Filipino landowning class. The incomes and the power of this Filipino class grew under American tenure, creating a type of political economy that we also encountered in the case of Argentina under British tutelage. American exports to the Philippines – mostly manufactured goods – also jumped sharply – nearly fivefold – between 1902 and 1920. And finally, with the security of a colonial government in place, American foreign investments into the Philippines also grew. Most of these went into mining; the output was again exported back to the USA. In sum, while the USA acquired the Philippines as a stepping stone to China, once colonized, it also served the important economic interests of the USA.

Beyond the Philippines lay China. That was the great prize all along. After winning the Spanish–American War, the USA became a Pacific power. With the Philippines as a base, the USA was now in a position to influence developments in China, though the American role in China was distinctly behind that of Britain and Japan. American interests in China were mainly commercial: the lure of the great China market. The USA wanted to promote trade with China and, if possible, facilitate private investments. These economic goals, however, immediately became political in so far as they required cooperating with other imperial powers in China on the one hand, and on the other hand, facilitating a degree of stability to the Qing monarchy. In order to prevent the carving up of china among imperial powers and to maintain access to the Chinese market, the USA promulgated the famous Open-Door Notes – a set of policy preferences – in 1899 and 1900. This policy was aimed mainly at other imperial powers active in China – as a matter of fact, the Chinese government was not even consulted about the merits of the policy – and urged them to cooperate so that the formal sovereignty of China could be maintained in a manner that would still ensure that the Chinese market remained open to all and sundry. The success of the Open-Door policies was limited. Yes, other imperial powers (save, Russia) paid lip-service to the idea of maintaining an open door to China, and American trade to China grew rapidly, tripling between 1900 and 1905. However, American preferences aside, Britain and Japan also went ahead to carve out their respective spheres of influence in China, and the Qing monarchy came undone in 1911, seriously interrupting American trade with China.

The significance of the Open-Door policies then lay, not in their immediate success, but elsewhere, namely, in helping us understand American motives and approach to opening peripheral markets. Following the Spanish–American War, the USA became a global power. Like Europe and Japan during the end of the age-of-empire century, the USA now sought access to markets and raw materials for its rapidly industrializing economy. Unlike Europe and Japan, however, the USA did not readily colonize other countries. America's anticolonial tradition was a factor, but so was America's competitive economy; what the USA needed were not exclusive colonial markets but open economies in which American firms could readily outcompete European and Japanese firms. An American approach to ensuring economic access to peripheral economies thus emerged via trial and error. Yes, it established a full colony in the Philippines and a near-colony in Cuba. However, a different approach of long-term significance was also evident in the case of China. With the Open-Door policies, the USA hoped to support the stability of the Qing monarchy on the one hand, but on the other hand, to also to keep it enfeebled enough so that the Chinese economy remained accessible to American economic interests. This approach to building an informal empire with peripheral governments that are stable but subservient is, of course, what the British had already been practicing in the nineteenth century, say, in the Ottoman Empire and Latin America. Now the USA also discovered this as a suitable approach that could combine American anticolonialism with economic imperialism; this was the making of an American approach to building an informal empire during the twentieth century. I will return to a discussion of post–World War II American imperialism after a brief discussion of Japanese imperialism that also unfolded in the first half of the twentieth century.

2.3 Japanese Imperialism

Toward the end of the nineteenth century, the Japanese joined the European powers and the USA in the imperial scramble for the available parts of the global periphery. The Scramble for Africa has already been discussed. Moreover, there was an uncanny resemblance in the pattern of American and Japanese expansion at the turn of the century. Just as the USA pried away Cuba and the Philippines from a decaying Spanish Empire, the Japanese took advantage of a weakening China and gobbled up Korea and Taiwan as formal colonies, and northeastern China as part of its informal empire. Were Japanese motives then similar or different than those of Britain and the USA during this time period? Historical evidence suggests that there are both similarities and differences but, in the end, what drove the Japanese to build a regional empire was the quest to enhance Japanese power, especially by strengthening Japanese economic links with the territories nearby; as in the case of Britain and the USA then, Japanese imperialism was also pushed by the need to pursue national prosperity and power, with a little more emphasis on power than on prosperity.

To recall a few historical facts, Japanese power had been growing since the Meiji transformation. More than British and American statesmen, Meiji oligarchs were overt economic nationalists. Japan had barely escaped being colonized; for Japan's leaders, economic modernization was essential as a means to preserve Japanese sovereignty against Western encroachments. They then used state power to promote industrialization and to build a powerful armed force at home. Japanese motives to expand overseas also emerged from this mind set. There is very little in the historical evidence to suggest that Japanese imperial expansion was pushed by emerging Japanese industrial or financial interests. However, it would also be absurd to separate security from economic interests in a case such as that of Meiji Japan. Meiji oligarchs were mercantilists of sorts; more than most, they thought of power as a means to promote economic modernization and, in turn, access more economic opportunities as a further source of national power.

Compared to the worldwide British Empire, Japan at the turn of the century sought only a regional empire. Russian expansionism and Britain's growing power over China posed a threat to Japanese regional ambitions. A disintegrating China in turn offered opportunities close to home, especially in China's client state, Korea. For an island country, Japanese leaders reasoned that Korea would provide a land base on the Asian continent. Korea – and through Korea, China – also offered economic opportunities. Meiji oligarchs understood that sustaining Japan's industrialization and economic growth would require expansion of foreign trade. If Western powers, including Russia, got in the way, Japan's economic prospects would be endangered. The same was the case in other economic arenas, such as promotion of banking and credit, securing concessions for mining and railroad construction, export of domestic capital, and expanding shipping (Duus, 1984, p. 137). Following the Opium Wars, Britain was already pursuing such economic activities in China. Russians, Americans and even Germans were keen to join the scramble for China. As a neighboring and rising power, Japan too entered the fray; it would have been surprising had it not. Geography gave Japan an advantage. Economic and military modernization enabled Japan to confront others, like the Russians, not to mention the decaying Chinese Empire. In quick order then, Japan established a colony in Taiwan following the Sino–Japanese War of 1895, replaced

China as a major influence over Korea, and then, following victory in the Russo–Japanese War in 1905, established a full colony in Korea in 1910, and established economic influence over northeastern provinces of China, especially Manchuria. I will return to a discussion of how the Japanese ruled Korea and the impact of Japanese colonialism in Section 4. For now, it is sufficient to reiterate that, in broad brushstrokes, Japanese imperialism too followed the British and American pattern of expansionism in search for economic opportunities and power overseas; however, as a regional power that had barely escaped colonial onslaught, national insecurity was a primary concern.

2.4 Post–World War II American Imperialism

The first half of the twentieth century was dominated by a world war, dissolution of old land empires, revolutions, economic depression, and then yet another world war. New patterns of imperialism only emerged following World War II, when the USA emerged as the world's most powerful country. America's power advantage over its nearest competitor, the Soviet Union, was sufficient for Americans to insist that they must get their way in the world "85 percent of the time."[8] The Americans then set out to create a global order that would enhance their own values and interests. The centerpiece of this new order was to be a world populated by capitalist countries, preferably democracies, embedded in an open global economy. With its competitive economy, the USA well understood that an open global economy will give American corporations a global edge that, in turn, will feed American prosperity and power. While many countries accepted – or were forced to accept – these American designs, not every one fell in line. A variety of communist and nationalist leaders in the world refused to accept a subordinate position in an American-led order: for example, Stalin sought to enhance the security of the Soviet Union by creating a land empire of closed economies in its neighborhood, thus precipitating the Cold War; the USA was unable to stop Mao Zedong and a communist revolution in China, thus feeding American insecurities about the spread of communism; and a variety of newly sovereign countries led by the likes of Jawaharlal Nehru (India), Soekarno (Indonesia), and Gamal Abdel Nasser (Egypt), sought to pursue state-led development that did not readily fit the American design of open economies.

Decolonization became a flood in the 1960s as many African countries also became formally sovereign. The Nkrumahs (Kwame Nkrumah, Ghana) and the Kenyattas (Jomo Kenyatta, Kenya) of Africa then joined the Nehrus and the Nassers in the nonaligned movement. As the Cold War heated, nonaligned countries sought to maintain an equidistance between the USA

---

[8] This statement was made by American president Harry S. Truman. See Leffler (1992), p. 15.

and the Soviet Union. The United Nations provided an umbrella for these newly created nations, providing an institutional voice for the importance of sovereignty and national self-determination as valued norms in global affairs. While no match for real military and economic power, for a time being, these norms helped new states consolidate their sovereignty. The USA often viewed the nonaligned block, especially countries like India and Egypt, with a degree of suspicion, both because of their commitment to statist economies and because of their vocal antiimperial nationalism. Some senior American decision-makers even considered the nonaligned as "closet commies." During the Cold War then, American internationalism came to be pitched against communism and developing country nationalism.

More than Britain in nineteenth century, the USA understood its global interests as a system of power; since parts are linked to the whole in any system, for the USA, weakness in any one part threatened the viability of the whole. When trying to understand the motives that drove American interventions in the developing world, it is important to keep this interconnected nature of the American Empire in mind; American interventions were often aimed at maintaining a system of global power, with open capitalist economies its centerpiece. And, as we will see, credibility of American commitments was the currency that was central to maintaining this informal empire. American priority during the Cold War was to encourage the rejuvenation of European capitalist democracies (and Japan), and to resist Soviet expansionism. The US approach to the developing world was shaped by these priorities. In the American post–World War II design, the developing world was to continue to provide raw materials and markets to advanced industrial economies, including to their former colonial masters, Britain, France, Japan, and even Belgium. This required that developing country economies be kept open. A variety of nationalists, who wanted to delink their economies from the global economy, were thus treated with suspicion. Soviet expansionism in the developing world was also to be contained. This, in turn, required that communists and left-of-center sympathizers of communists within the developing world be tamed. With the goal of an open global economy, a variety of nationalists and communists thus came to bear the brunt of American power. Most of the American interventions in the developing world that I review– albeit in brief – can be understood from this standpoint.

Early in the Cold War, the USA intervened to covertly replace democratically elected nationalist leaders with pro-American autocrats as rulers in disparate countries such as Iran and Guatemala.[9] While the rhetoric used to legitimize

---

[9] For the American-sponsored coup in Iran, see Abrahamian (2013), and for Guatemala, Grandin (2000).

these CIA-sponsored coups was the threat of communism, historical evidence has subsequently clarified that the prospect of communist takeover in these cases – as well as in the case of Chile – was minimal; the real motives that drove American interventions lay elsewhere. For example, prior to World War II, American interests in Iran were minimal. Russia and Britain had vied for influence over a fragmented Iran instead. British influence over Iran was especially significant because they owned much of Iranian oil; oil extraction and exports, in turn, were of great importance to Britain, especially following World War II, when the British economy was in tatters and in desperate need of foreign exchange. At the same time, however, this was also the period when a variety of colonies and near-colonies were demanding full sovereignty. Iran was no exception. Under the leadership of an Iranian nationalist – Mohammed Mossadegh – Iranians demanded control over their major economic resource, oil. After being elected the prime minister of Iran in 1952, Mossadegh nationalized the British-owned Anglo-Iranian Oil company; for the Iranians, this was equivalent to decolonization. Oil nationalization, in turn, set up the conflict between Britain and Iran that was eventually "resolved" only with the US-sponsored overthrow of Mossadegh.

A number of interrelated concerns moved the Americans to sponsor a coup in Iran that overthrew Mossadegh and replaced him with the pro-American Shah of Iran as the ruler of that country. First, following World War II, the economic recovery of Britain was a priority for the Americans; a variety of American economic programs, including the Marshall plan, were aimed to reconstruct Western Europe. The USA wanted to promote American exports to Western European countries but Britain had limited foreign exchange. Britain had just lost India and now, with the loss of oil revenues from Iran looming, the USA stepped in to help Britain maintain some of its colonial-type links. Of course, such help did not come without a price; after the nationalization was reversed under the Shah's leadership, American companies secured a healthy chunk of Iranian oil. Second, a legitimate case could be made at the time that, given its geography, Iran could readily come under Soviet threat. The British made such a case to the Americans and the Americans, in turn, used the rhetoric of anticommunism to build support among the American political class for the CIA-sponsored coup. With the Korean War on, and McCarthyism growing in the USA, American decision-makers did not want to be seen "losing" yet another country to communism. However, it is clear by now that, at that time, the Soviet-supported Tudeh party had neither the intention nor the capacity to play a major role in Iranian politics; and, more importantly, both the British and American decision-makers were aware of these limitations of Iranian communists. And finally, the USA was keen during this period to set up global norms as to who controlled natural resources in the developing world. The US-sponsored coup in Guatemala in 1954, for example, overthrew Jacobo Árbenz, a social-democratic leader, who sought to nationalize Guatemalan land owned by such foreign corporations as the United Fruit Company. This was aimed as much at further-ing the narrow interests of an American corporation as it was an announcement to all and sundry that such nationalizations will not be tolerated. The coup against Mossadegh similarly sought to establish the norm that nationalization of foreign corporations in the developing world will be resisted, strongly. This too was the new American order in the making.

Parallel to the USA stepping into British imperial shoes in Iran, the USA in the post–World War II period also intervened in Vietnam to first support, and then supplant, French imperialism. This early intervention of course led to a quarter-century war in Vietnam that killed nearly three million Vietnamese. The causes and consequences of the US intervention in Vietnam are a complex set of issues that have been debated extensively.[10] For the purposes of this section, it is important to note that American motives evolved: Following World War II, the USA first wanted to support the economic recovery of France, and to an extent Japan; then, the USA sought to stabilize a noncommunist South Vietnam so as to stop the economically valuable Southeast Asian dominoes from falling to communism; and eventually, even when it became clear that the Vietnamese were no stooges of China or the Soviet Union, the USA continued its war against Vietnam so as to preserve its "credibility" as the leader of the capitalist world.

French colonial rule in Vietnam was brutal and exploitative. The colonial economy of Vietnam was also lucrative for the French in so far as it absorbed French manufactured goods, provided cheap raw materials, and was a steady source of foreign exchange. The Japanese threw the French out of Vietnam during World War II but they too, in turn, were thrown out when they lost World War II. Ho Chi Minh then declared Vietnam independent. At this critical moment, instead of recognizing Vietnam as a sovereign state, the USA tacitly allowed the French to reenter Vietnam. The reasoning was that, following World War II, France remained a junior ally of the Americans; recovery of war-torn European economies – and Japan – was now an American priority. And as in the case of the British in Iran, American policy-makers during the Truman administration reasoned that France will need its colonies, such as Vietnam, for its economic recovery. Control of Vietnam thus came to be increasingly con-tested between Vietnamese nationalist forces led by Ho Chi Minh and the French colonial forces. In this classic struggle between colonialism and

---

[10] The best book on the American war in Vietnam is still Young (1991).

nationalism, the USA started supporting the French militarily; by 1953, the USA bore nearly a third of the cost of France's anticolonial war. However, as is well known, the French eventually lost this colonial war against the Vietnamese in 1954 at Dien Bien Phu. Early American intervention in Vietnam was thus very much aimed at helping the economic recovery of a crucial European ally.

Following the military defeat of France, Vietnam was divided into a northern and a southern half, with a tacit agreement among major powers – formalized as the Geneva Accords – that democratic elections will follow to create a new government for a unified Vietnam. However, the USA was a major power in southern Vietnam by now. Fearing Ho Chi Minh's electoral victory, the USA during the Eisenhower years did not allow democratic elections to proceed. Instead, the division of Vietnam hardened. From then on, the USA sought to create a sovereign, noncommunist South Vietnam and the northern communist government sought to unify the country under their leadership. The two decades of warfare that followed was essentially around this fault line. During the 1950s, American leaders worried that the victory of communism in Vietnam would lead to communist victories in much of Southeast Asia and beyond. The region was considered economically valuable, especially to support Japan's economic recovery, but also more broadly, as a source of valuable raw materials and an outlet for industrial goods. In order to prevent dominoes from collapsing, the USA started to pour more and more resources into South Vietnam, first to build its state and economy, and when those efforts failed, by sending American troops directly to do the job.

US troops in Vietnam started increasing during the Kennedy years and then escalated sharply under Lyndon B. Johnson. Thereafter, US troop levels declined, but aerial bombing increased dramatically instead, when Richard Nixon and Henry Kissinger sought "peace with honor," and got neither. The USA eventually pulled out of Vietnam in 1973 and the northern communists recaptured southern Vietnam in 1975, marking a colossal failure of American imperial efforts to shape a country half way around the world. While the ups and downs of American policies were obviously a reaction to a host of developments, both Johnson and Nixon argued that one important reason to continue the war in Vietnam – even when it was clear that the war was not winnable – was to maintain American credibility. The underlying reasoning was rooted in America's self-defined role as a global power. With client states the world over, credibility of American commitments was the currency to maintain a global informal empire. If clients did not take American commitments seriously, then the goal of eliciting subservience – without overt use of force – would be endangered. Hence, it was argued *ad nauseam* during the Vietnam years, that the USA must stabilize its "offspring," South Vietnam; only when this goal was met, would others take America's global role seriously. In sum, while American motives in Vietnam started out as supportive of the economic recovery of France and Japan, over time, they morphed into drawing a line to stop communist expansion, and finally into an exercise in maintaining a global system of power – America's informal empire.

As the USA was losing the war in Vietnam, it decided to intervene closer to home in Chile to stop the possible spread of a socialist model of development in Latin America.[11] The USA has long considered Latin America its "backyard," or a region in which American influence ought to hold sway. Following the Cuban revolution, the USA had sought to tame left opposition forces in Latin America via a variety of pathways, including sponsoring a developmentally oriented regional program, the Alliance for Progress, training military officers of various countries, and supporting right-of-center autocrats that promised to maintain "order" in their respective countries. Chile was of special concern to the USA because it had a long tradition of democratic politics, as well as a vibrant left. Even before Salvador Allende's electoral victory in 1970, the USA had covertly aided antileft political forces in Chile. When these efforts failed, and the socialist Allende became Chile's president, Nixon and Kissinger ordered the CIA to derail his presidency, an effort that led to the death of Allende and the instalment of the brutal dictator Augusto Pinochet in power.

Why did the USA intervene in Chile? Nixon and Kissinger argued that Allende had to be deposed because he was a communist in cahoots with the Soviet Union. Subsequent evidence has clarified – and the American intelligence community understood this at the time – that Soviet influence on Allende was minimal. As in the case of the coup against Mossadegh in Iran, the anticommunist rhetoric against Allende served as a convenient bogeyman during the Cold War. The real issue was that Allende was a left-leaning Chilean nationalist who wanted to reduce Chile's economic dependency and redistribute resources at home. After coming to power, Allende's main policies included land redistribution within Chile and the nationalization of select foreign corporations, including American companies that extracted and exported Chile's key export, copper. Both the Chilean upper classes and the Nixon administration in the USA reacted sharply. What was at stake were both narrow economic interests of select economic elite but also the broader threat that Allende's success in Chile may encourage such nationalistic moves in other Latin American countries. What the USA needed in Latin America were subservient leaders who would quietly pursue policies favorable to American economic interests. Allende's nationalist and socialist model of development challenged these imperial ambitions – he had to go. The coup that overthrew the democratically elected

---

[11] A good study of American intervention in Chile is Kornbluh (2004).

Salvador Allende was then very much reminiscent of the earlier US-sponsored coups in such countries as Iran, Guatemala, and Congo.

If a security threat posed by the Soviet Union was the primary motive behind American interventions during the Cold War, there should have been a pronounced decline in such interventions in the post–Cold War period. As we know, this was not the case. American economic and military interventions in the global periphery have become even more brazen – and overt – since the dissolution of the Soviet Union; it is as if there were no checks left on American power in a unipolar world to try to shape developing countries in its own interests. But what are these interests? A brief discussion of American efforts to forcibly alter economic policies in the developing world, especially in Latin America, under the rubric of the Washington Consensus, and military interventions in the Middle East, such as the two wars in Iraq, will help us understand how economic forces are continuing to drive American imperialism.

Toward the end of the twentieth century, the center of gravity of the American economy shifted from manufacturing to finance. This trend began during the 1960s, with the post–World War II reemergence of Japan and Germany as manufacturing power houses, then accelerated with the export success, first of such smaller countries as South Korea and Taiwan in the 1970s, and eventually, of course, China. Meanwhile, the global prowess of American banks had grown during the 1970s; among the reasons for this was ready access to oil money from the Organization of the Petroleum Exporting Countries (OPEC) during the 1970s. Flush with unregulated money – in offshore branches – American banks then lent heavily to developing countries, especially in Latin America. Many Latin American countries during this period were ruled by authoritarian rulers committed to economic growth. The implicit quid pro quo was that American banks would help finance the growth of such countries as Brazil, Argentina, and Mexico, then, with growth and exports, these countries in turn will readily pay back their loans, completing a benign loop. Unfortunately, several developments undermined these optimistic calculations, especially decisions within the USA to increase short-term interest rates. The debt burden of many Latin American countries then rose sharply and the 1980s turned into a decade of debt crisis.

At the heart of the debt crisis of the 1980s were some one dozen highly exposed American banks and half a dozen highly indebted Latin American countries. The American approach to the debt crisis was to portray it as potentially a global financial crisis that the USA was intervening to avert. In actuality, these American interventions were aimed first and foremost at ensuring that American banks did not suffer; these banks were by now the dynamic core of the American economy. Americans channeled money directly as well as indirectly – via the International Monetary Fund (IMF), where the USA exercises disproportionate influence – to ensure that Latin American countries had enough foreign exchange to continue to service their debts to American banks. The short-term crisis for the banks was thus averted but Latin American countries became even more indebted, needing to borrow yet more to service the debt. As a condition for these loans, the USA then continued to pressure Latin American countries to change their economic policies so as to generate foreign exchange savings to service their debt. These policies came to be dubbed the Washington Consensus on development – or structural adjustment policies – and included such demands as cutting budget deficits, privatizing state firms, opening the economy to foreign goods and investments, and more generally, getting prices right. There were doubts at the highest policy-making levels – especially in Latin America but also in American policy-making circles, including in the World Bank – that structural adjustment policies may not generate economic growth in Latin American countries.[12] And yet, these policies were still imposed on Latin American countries because they would ensure debt repayment to banks, as well as open Latin American economies to American goods and investors. I will return in Section 4 to discuss the impact of these American policies on Latin America.

In addition to the soft imperialism of the type that imposing the Washington Consensus represented, the USA in the post–Cold War period also undertook hard imperialism of forced regime change in such Middle East countries as Iraq.[13] With its vast oil resources, the Middle East has been of great interest to Western powers for much of the twentieth century, first Britain and then the USA. Once British power in the region waned in the post–World War II period, the USA used its client states – Iran under the Shah, and Saudi Arabia with its dependent monarch – as proxy powers to preserve its interests in the region. The Islamic revolution in Iran in 1979, however, heralded major changes. Since then, the USA became involved directly, with a significant military presence in the region.[14] The USA sought to shape intraregional politics, aimed at both ensuring the security of Israel and preventing the emergence of a regional hegemon; hence, the USA supported Saddam Hussein against Iran in the Iran–Iraq War of the 1980s. With the decline of the Soviet Union, the USA felt further emboldened to shape the region in its own image. The two American wars in Iraq have to be understood within this context.

---

[12] See, for example, Stiglitz (2003).

[13] The case of Afghanistan could also be included here. I chose not to discuss it because the US intervention in Afghanistan was less imperialistic in the sense of the word used here but more a war-of-vengeance following 9/11. While American failure at nation-building in Afghanistan can be compared usefully to other such failures, as in South Vietnam – and I will return to some such issues in a subsequent section – American motives in Afghanistan were somewhat sui generis.

[14] See, Bacevich (2016).

When Saddam Hussein foolishly – and brazenly – annexed Kuwait, the USA unleashed its military fury. Saddam was quickly defeated and the "sovereignty" of Kuwait was restored. What drove Americans to intervene in Iraq in 1991 was relatively clear: a potentially hostile dictator could not be allowed to control the vast oil fields of Kuwait; and, if in the process, the norms of national self-determination could be further reaffirmed, that was icing on the cake. After that swift military victory, Iraq under Saddam Hussein was pretty well a contained power. Why the USA intervened again in 2003 then remains somewhat of a mystery. Though the war formally ended in 2011, when most US troops pulled out, American efforts to shape Iraq continue. Meanwhile, half a million Iraqis have died during American efforts to "liberate" Iraq.

Among the motives that drove America's imperial war in Iraq, the least persuasive was the official rationale, namely, that Saddam possessed weapons of mass destruction; no such weapons were ever found. The suggestion by some that the war was about Iraq's oil or about enhancing Israel's security are also not persuasive. Iraq's oil was already available in the global market and Saddam Hussein was even willing to invite foreign investors to invest in its oil fields. And Saddam's weakened Iraq was no military threat to the nuclear-armed Israel in 2002. The murky motives that drove the Bush administration to invade Iraq for the second time were rooted instead in the euphoria that engulfed American decision-makers at the end of the Cold War. In a unipolar world, with American power seemingly unchallenged, the USA wished to remake the parts of the world that mattered the most to it. We have already noticed the rolling back of the state in Latin America under the rubric of Washington Consensus. The oil-rich Middle East was high on the American wish list for restructuring, even before 9/11, and within the Middle East, Saddam Hussein was also high on the list to go because he was ambitious and sat atop a lot of oil wealth. Just as important: Toppling Saddam and remaking Iraq into an open democratic and capitalist economy was a dream that appealed to many in the Bush administration; for example, in the words of Condoleezza Rice, cherished American goals ought not to "stop at the edge of Islam."[15] So, the second war in Iraq was to be a first step in a much more ambitious project to establish some sort of *Pax Americana* over the oil-rich Middle East. That it has not worked out as hoped does not take anything away from how and why it started; the same was the case in Vietnam.

2.5 Conclusion

Scholarly disagreements about why metropolitan powers imperialize are well rehearsed. Unfortunately, many of these arguments are either derived from, or are

---

[15] Interview in the *Financial Times*, September 22, 2002.

supported by, a narrow set of cases. Surprisingly, the Scramble for Africa at the end of the nineteenth century has played a significant role in shaping the theoretical debates that pitch the Hobson–Lenin type of economic arguments against a variety of scholars that embrace a *real politik* perspective. My suggestion here instead is that a vast array of instances of imperialism can more readily be interpreted as efforts of metropolitan states to enhance national economic prosperity. Metropolitan states do so by prying open peripheral economies that in turn provides new economic opportunities for the capitalists of core economies.

Among the cases reviewed here, albeit in brief, British colonialism in India, and Britain's informal empire in Argentina and China fit this suggestion readily. By contrast, Britain's expansion into Egypt, as well as the related Scramble for Africa, combined both political and economic motives; very often, however, as in the case of British colonialism in Nigeria, the power conflict, say with France, was very much about who gets ready access to peripheral markets. Japanese expansion was also similar; while security concerns were important, new economic opportunities as a further source of power provided the broader context. The motives that drove American expansionism in the global periphery were economic too but differed from that of Britain because the USA was a giant, continent-sized economy; while Britain needed an empire to sustain its economic dynamism at home, the USA merely wanted one. Over time, of course, seeking economic opportunities in peripheral economies became a habit for Americans too. Of the cases examined, early American expansion into the Philippines, Cuba, and other central American countries, as well as into China, were very much driven by economic needs. The interventions during the Cold War were a little more complicated, especially in a case like Vietnam, where the threat of communism was real, but in such other cases as Iran, Guatemala, Congo, and Chile, the rhetoric of anticommunism provided a cloak for the pursuit of economic interests, both of the narrow kind that benefitted select American corporations and broader goals of enhancing national prosperity. The same very much holds true in the cases of post–Cold War interventions: when American banks were rescued at the expense of Latin American countries, and military intervention in Iraq was pursued as a first step in some grandiose goal of establishing American domination over the oil-rich Middle East.

3 Strategies of Imperialism

The metropolitan project of prying open peripheral economies never came with a manual on how to do so. Strategies of imperialism have thus evolved, often via trial and error, reacting to differing circumstances at both home and abroad. In this brief section, I discuss some of the major variations in strategies of imperialism: formal versus informal empire; variations within how informal empires were set up; and some major differences between the British and the American modes of imperialism. These variations are important to understand, not only for the obvious reason that they help make sense of some of the differing patterns of imperialism, but also because alternate strategies bequeathed differing long-term legacies. We will visit the issue of the economic and political legacies of imperialism for the developing world in the next section.

3.1 Formal versus Informal Empire

Why did metropolitan powers choose to establish formal territorial control – colonies – in some parts of the world, but settled for an informal empire in other parts of the world? The choice between establishing formal or informal control was more serious for Britain in the nineteenth century than it was for the Americans in the twentieth. By the time that the USA became a global power in the mid-twentieth century, it was rather "late" in history to establish anew a far-flung colonial empire; colonialism had been deeply delegitimized by the emergence and the success of various nationalist movements across European colonies. I will return to this issue of why the Americans – for the most part – came to prefer informal over formal empire. But for the British, the choice was real. They established important colonies like India prior to the nineteenth century. Then, with the rise of industrial capitalism in the nineteenth century, they came to prefer informal empire in such disparate but significant places as Latin America, China, and the Ottoman Empire. It may then be tempting to suggest that the shift from mercantilism to capitalism might help explain these shifting strategies from the eighteenth to the nineteenth century. However, historical complexities then muddy analytical parsimony: Toward the end of the nineteenth century, Britain (and other industrializing, capitalist economies) again burst upon the global scene to carve up much of the remaining open spaces in the world – such as in Africa – into their respective colonies. So, how does one understand these shifting preferences between formal and informal empire?

British historians Gallagher and Robinson (1953) argued that, for the most part, Britain preferred an informal empire – imperialism of free trade – in the nineteenth century, but resorted to territorial conquest when gunboat diplomacy failed to create favorable conditions. There is merit in this argument, but it requires qualifications. Even in the nineteenth century, British preference for informal empire was hardly universal. For example, consider the most important case of Britain in India. Prior to the nineteenth century, when the mercantilist East

India Company was establishing rule over India in the eighteenth century, no one in Britain debated if an informal empire would suffice instead. The British wanted territorial control over India from the outset; it was Indian land revenues that contributed handsomely to the profitability of the Raj in the eighteenth century. Intensive taxation of Indian agriculture in turn would not have been possible without substantial state power. The British in India thus created a large armed force to control Indians. They also established a large civil service, at least in part to help collect land revenues. The armed force and the civil service in turn came to be the heart of an autocratic colonial state. All of this is consistent with a view that hard colonialism was a product of the age of mercantilism. However, even with the rise of capitalism, the British approach to India hardly softened; if anything, it hardened even further. When Britain faced a major revolt in India in the mid-nineteenth century, there was little debate in Britain over the merits of holding on to India; India was far too profitable to let go. The British did debate – even incessantly – whether to rule the Indian colony more or less directly,[16] but seldom to give it any real political autonomy. The British crushed the Indian revolt instead and established Crown rule over India, declaring Queen Victoria the Empress of India. So, for those who argue that the rise of capitalism and free trade in the nineteenth century weakened the British colonial urge, the Indian case provides a real analytical conundrum.

In other parts of the world, the British in the nineteenth century indeed came to prefer informal over formal empire. Why? Lord Palmerston, a key architect of British foreign policy in the nineteenth century, once remarked that economies at the global periphery should be "well kept" and "always accessible," and as long as they were, territorial conquest was not needed.[17] This really is the heart of the matter. The British choice of formal versus informal empire in the nineteenth century depended on how readily the British could secure stability – well kept – and subservience – always accessible – in peripheral countries. Since conditions varied, so did British strategy; as long as British power was unchallenged and its economy competitive, informal empire provided a viable alternative to colonialism. Following the Napoleonic Wars, for example, British power, especially naval power, was nearly unchallenged. In Latin America, the Spaniards and the Portuguese lost their colonies as a result of these wars, and, for the most part, Britain could also keep the French and the USA out of the region. British power of course rested on a rapidly industrializing economy;

---

[16] The debates about how directly – or indirectly – to rule a colony were different than debates over whether to establish a formal colony or informal domination.

[17] This comment was made with reference to Egypt, and at the time, Palmerston was expressing a preference for an informal over formal empire in Egypt, a desire that of course crumbled toward the end of the century. See, for example, https://libquotes.com/henry-temple.

Britain was by now emerging as the workshop of the world. With paramount power and a competitive economy, the British then sought to expand into Latin America. The issue of whether to establish colonies in the region was considered but set aside; establishing colonies would have met resistance from the creole ruling class, as well as possibly from the USA. Moreover, colonies were really not needed because the main interest in the region was to open it up for economic penetration. Since other European powers could be kept out, the main challenge of economic expansion in the region could be met by helping establish stable-but-subservient rulers in power. The examples of Brazil and Argentina help us understand this "easy" pathway to informal empire.

In a country like Brazil, the transition to a stable-but-subservient rule was relatively smooth. This was because the dependent Portuguese emperor willingly moved to Brazil under British protection, and, in turn, the Brazilian elite readily accepted him as their ruler. Such were the beginnings of Brazil's short nineteenth century under British tutelage. The power of the monarchy was constrained, with dependence on the British from the outside, but also due to pressures from powerful regional overlords on the inside. In spite of nominal sovereignty, therefore, the Brazilian state did not develop much of a centralized character during the nineteenth century; those developments came only in the early twentieth century, when the British influence waned and regional resistance was overcome by urban middle classes, including the military. Meanwhile, during the nineteenth century, the weak emperor granted the British rights to sell their goods to Brazil, while slapping tariffs on those of others. British manufactured goods then came to dominate the Brazilian marketplace for much of the century. The British also eventually built Brazilian railroads, the profits of which were guaranteed by the monarchial state. Brazilian commodity exports, in turn, went through booms and busts, but were sufficient to sustain a powerful land-owning oligarchy. This export-oriented ruling class supported open economy arrangements that served both their and British interests well, though at the expense of retarding the development of Brazil as a modern, industrial economy. Whenever some nationalist elements within Brazil sought protectionism for the economy, or demanded that the government be more centralized, capable of raising more revenues, British political pressure ensured that such moves did not come to pass. Though nominally a sovereign country then, Brazil for much of the century was "in fact … a British colony" (Graham, 1969).

Britain had more trouble establishing dominance over Argentina than in Brazil, but once established, British power in Argentina came to be even more pronounced than in Brazil during the nineteenth century. Britain periodically used force, especially during the first half of the century, to help establish governments in power that would facilitate stability, encourage trade and investments with Britain, and ensure that British loans to Argentina were paid back. British interventions included keeping other powers like France and Spain out via the use of naval blockades, as well as shaping Argentinian politics by encouraging one faction to power here, threatening another faction there, and eventually helping consolidate a federal polity in which rural and provincial interests had a prominent place. Gunboats ensured the political arrangements needed to establish an informal empire. Thereafter, the complementarities between the economies of Britain and Argentina grew. Land-abundant Argentina provided farm products to Britain, and Britain, in turn, provided a variety of manufactured goods to Argentina's ruling classes. Compared to Brazil, the Argentinian economy also grew rather well under British tutelage. An Argentinian upper class of ranchers, merchants, and politicians benefitted from this type of dependent development, but again, at the expense of the masses; what was also sacrificed was the long-term prospects of an industrial or, at least, a more diversified economy.

Compared to Latin America, Britain's informal empire in Egypt and China required more overt use of force. This is because, for the most part, ruling groups in Latin America were fellow Europeans, who benefitted from dependent development within the frame of Britain's informal empire; Britain did use force in Latin America, but sparingly and intermittently. By contrast, both Egypt and China were ancient civilizations, with a strong sense of self; their rulers resisted European encroachment but eventually succumbed to superior force. Britain's informal empire in Egypt and China thus help us understand the range of approaches that the British used to build their informal empire, with varying long-term legacies.

The case of Britain in Egypt is telling in so far as it underlines that the British during the nineteenth century did whatever it took to keep their client states pliable and lucrative. During the first half of the century, for example, when Mohammed Ali sought to modernize the Egyptian economy and its armed forces, the British imposed a free trade treaty on the struggling Ottoman Empire, including on its Egyptian province, undercutting his ambitions. This also opened up Egypt to British manufacturing goods and slowly but surely turned Egypt into a large cotton plantation that served the British market. Over time, as infrastructure projects led to unpaid loans, British imperial strategy shifted from mere free trade treaties to direct participation in the Egyptian government to ensure the repayment of debts. When nationalistic Egyptians revolted – for example, the Urabi Revolt, 1879–1882 – the British again recalibrated their imperial strategy; they used superior military force to crush the revolt. Egypt thus became a near-colony of Britain in the post-1882 period, with a British viceroy of sorts in direct control. This was also the beginning of the broader Scramble for Africa. What this imperial pathway of one-thing-led-to-another in Egypt suggests is that the British during the nineteenth century settled for an informal empire when they could, but then readily moved to more formal colonialism when informal control did not suffice.[18]

The contrasting approach of Britain to China and India at the mid-century also sheds light on the broader issue of the circumstances under which Britain chose formal versus informal empire. While no one in Britain questioned the need to hold on to its Indian colony at the mid-century, the issue of whether China should also be colonized was considered but, as in the case of Latin America, was quickly set aside. Why? By the mid-century, much of the difficult task of conquering a fragmented India had already been accomplished by the Crown-supported East India Company. By contrast, conquering a moderately well-functioning Qing empire would have required an enormous military and bureaucratic effort. Such an effort was also not needed. Britain's main interest in China was economic, specifically trade; unlike Egypt, China was not on the way to anywhere. British authorities reasoned that what was needed in China instead of a full-blown colony was a stable-but-subservient government that would keep the Chinese economy open for business. When Chinese authorities resisted, the infamous Opium Wars followed. British military superiority in turn facilitated the establishment of an informal empire for much of the second half of the nineteenth century. Throughout this period, British efforts were then aimed at propping up the faltering Qing monarchy on the one hand, and on the other hand, imposing a variety of onerous terms and treaties on China that generated handsome economic benefits for both British merchants and the British state.

Britain's informal empire in China draws attention to two somewhat peripheral but related issues that shed further light on the question at hand, namely, the circumstances that led to formal versus informal empire. First, alongside the British, the other major power in China from late nineteenth century onward was of course Japan. Japan colonized Korea and Taiwan in the early twentieth century but chose to establish informal empire over parts of China. Why? Japan's main interest in China was economic: trade and investment. Many powers were competing for similar opportunities in China. Had Japan sought to establish formal colonialism over parts of China, Britain and other powers, including the USA, would have surely resisted. As a regional power, Japan was in no position to undertake such adventures against Western powers, certainly not in the early twentieth century. More important, what Japan wanted in

---

[18] It may be worth noting that the argument of Gallagher and Robinson (1953) rests heavily on the Egyptian case.

China – economic access – it could have via informal sharing of China among competing powers. It was only when China's disintegration proceeded further, say, in the 1930s, that Japanese aims in China again turned more militaristic, toward occupation and territorial control.

The second important issue that the case of Britain in China highlights is how the emerging contention among imperialist powers to divide up the spoils was to be handled. During the second half of the nineteenth century, industrializing Japan posed a special threat to British interests in China. Russia, Germany, and the USA also joined the fray. As in the case of Scramble for Africa, one may ask: Why did imperialist powers not divide up China into a number of colonies? To an extent they did, but the division remained informal, with spheres of influence. Unlike Africa, China was never fully colonized. Had China been divided into a number of colonies, scholars will surely suggest – as they do for Scramble for Africa – that competion among rival imperial powers led to a scramble for China. However, what the Chinese case underlines instead is that there was an alternate pathway to deal with imperialist rivalries, a pathway that proved to be of greater long-term significance than the division of Africa among rival imperial powers. This was the pathway of cooperation among imperialist powers to keep China unified but weak and subservient, available for all imperialist powers to exploit. Over time, the Americans called this the Open-Door policy, an early example of multilateral cooperation aimed at establishing an open economy imperium. What is worth noting for the present discussion then is this: There was nothing inevitable about interimperial rivalries driving a new wave of colonialism at the end of the nineteenth century. Such rivalries were real, but they led to informal division of China on the one hand, but on the other hand, to a formal division of sub-Saharan Africa. Surely, the explanation for British preference for formal empire in some places but informal empire elsewhere does not lie mainly with growing imperial rivalries.

If so, how does one best understand Britain's shift back to full blown colonialism toward the end of the nineteenth century, especially in sub-Saharan Africa? Growing rivalries among industrializing powers were indeed one factor, but that was far from the full story. As noted already, it is also important to keep in mind the changing economic context of these rivalries. A number of developments enhanced European economic interest in Africa toward the end of the century: reduction in shipping costs; the prospect of linking interiors to the coast via railways; and medical developments that enabled Europeans to live and pursue profits in tropical conditions. Why could these new economic opportunities in Africa not be readily pursued within the framework of an informal empire? The functioning of an informal empire requires stable-subservience in peripheral countries; such an arrangement in turn presupposes some sort of state-like structures and a collaborating ruling elite. These conditions were absent in much of sub-Saharan Africa. Unlike China or the Ottoman Empire, for example, there were no established large-scale political units in the region. And unlike Latin America also, there were no influential land-owning classes that might become active collaborators. Subservient states would have to be created anew in the region. And this need in turn favored full-blown colonial control over territories. In sum, growing economic importance of Africa, and difficulties of pursuing these economic opportunities without formal control, pushed intra-European rivalries toward the colonial division of Africa.

To conclude this discussion on choice of formal versus informal empire, the simple point that ought to be reiterated is that the purpose of imperialism was to take economic advantage of peripheral countries. What was needed politically to pursue such goals was a stable but subservient periphery. When stability was absent, this encouraged the establishment of formal control; British colonialism over both fragmented India in the eighteenth century and Nigeria at the end of the nineteenth century support this proposition. When competing powers also wanted a share of the imperial pie, this in turn encouraged the spoils to be carved up, such as during the Scramble for Africa. In between these cases of early and late colonialism – during much of the nineteenth century, when Britain's political and economic hegemony was unchallenged – informal empire offered an alternative, cost-effective approach to economic penetration of peripheral countries. When local rulers could maintain stability and were willing to cooperate, say, in Brazil and Argentina, the result was easy informal empire – that is, without the use of excessive force. By contrast, the cases of China and Egypt underline that the British were more than willing to bludgeon rulers who resisted economic opening; informal – or even near-formal – empire then followed. In sum, the choice of formal versus informal empire reflected the differing circumstances under which the British could secure stability and subservience in a peripheral country.

3.2 Pathways to Informal Empire

While Britain in its heyday pursued both formal and informal empire, the American approach to building influence over the Global South has been mainly informal. Of course, it did not start out that way. As discussed earlier, following the Spanish–American War, the USA used hard military force to turn the Philippines into a formal colony and Cuba into a near-colony. Viewed over the long American twentieth century, however, the American way of empire has mainly eschewed formal colonialism. A number of factors help us understand why. *First*, by the time that the USA became a global player in the early twentieth century, much of the developing world was already colonized; if the USA wanted a share of the Global South, it would have had to fight the likes of Britain and France. And this was really not needed. The American economy was getting increasingly competitive vis-à-vis the Europeans. What the USA needed was open access to developing country markets, not territorial control. *Second*, America's anticolonial tradition played a part; the reluctance to establish full colonies was evident in the debates between "imperialists" and "antiimperialists" in the context of the Spanish–American War, especially in debates over what to do with Cuba following that war. Woodrow Wilson then associated the USA with a commitment to "self-determination" of nations. While this commitment served important *real politik* interests at the time – it undermined the power of old empires – the rhetorical commitment also put some real constraints on colonialism as a strategy of American expansion. *Third*, following World War II, anticolonial nationalist movements succeeded in numerous parts of the "Third World"; norms of anticolonialism then became embedded in institutions like the United Nations – that the USA at the time supported. And finally, with the emergence of the Cold War, efforts to nakedly subjugate one developing country or another would have probably cost the USA support among other developing countries, helping the Soviet Union in the process. Of course, this did not stop the USA from intervening when the perceived stakes were high, say, in Iran, Guatemala, Congo, Vietnam, or Chile. The goal of such interventions was nevertheless never to establish full colonies; it was rather to establish pro-American client states that would facilitate stability and subservience. This pattern of establishing influence over the Global South then persisted into the post–Cold War period, with mixed results.

The American approach to building an informal empire has followed three different pathways: hard militarism; covert regime change; and multilateral domination. The issue that is worth discussing in brief then is: Why American strategies for establishing influence in the Global South have varied? The USA used significant military power to subjugate and shape such countries of the Global South as the Philippines at the turn of the century, Vietnam during the Cold War, and more recently, Afghanistan and Iraq. What do such cases of hard militarism have in common? Two conditions stand out: On the one hand, the perceived stakes in all of these cases were high but nebulous; on the other hand, indigenous opposition to American goals in all of these cases was strong. So, the Philippines was to be the gateway to the celebrated China market, but Filipino nationalists put up significant resistance to American colonialism. Vietnam became the line where communist dominoes were to stop falling, but Vietnamese communists and nationalists proved to be formidable foes.

Afghanistan had to be tamed so no more attacks would be launched from its soil on America, and yet the Taliban too proved to be insurmountable. And finally, military intervention in Iraq was to be a first step in the much broader – and quixotic – goal of establishing *Pax Americana* over the oil-rich Middle East, but neither Saddam Hussein nor a variety of other Iraqi nationalist groups readily succumbed.

Whether the USA succeeded in its military interventions or not – and more often, especially in recent periods, it has not – the decision-making calculus leading up to such interventions followed this logic: The perception was that significant American interests were at stake in a developing country but local nationalists stood firmly in the way. American policy-makers then decided to tame the recalcitrant nationalists via hard militarism. Earlier British efforts to create an informal empire also followed a somewhat similar logic. We thus noticed that when local elites were willing to cooperate, say, in Brazil and Argentina, the British did not need to use much force to establish its informal empire. By contrast, both Egypt and China were harder nuts to crack in the nineteenth century. The stakes in both cases were high – economic in China, and both political and economic in Egypt – but local rulers did not readily submit to British goals. Hard militarism followed.

Covert regime change is the second route that Americans have pursued widely to establish its influence over peripheral countries. The goal has been the same as it was in cases of hard militarism, namely, to establish pro-American regimes that will maintain political stability and pursue policies desired by Americans. Covert regime change is clearly a less costly strategy to orchestrate a regime change in a developing country than a full-blown war. It tends to emerge as the preferred strategy when such conditions hold: American interests in a specific country are clear, often protecting economic interests, and the power differential between the USA and the smaller power is significant. The USA has thus pursued this route to an informal empire most often in its backyard: Central and South America. American power over these countries is considerable, not only because the USA is a military giant, but also because American investments in these countries tends to be large and the USA has often trained their militaries. All of these power resources provide considerable leverage to the USA over these countries. So, when a nationalist of sorts comes to power in one of these countries, especially one who wishes to pursue a development path that American decision-makers deem undesirable, the wheels of covert regime change go into motion. Even following the Spanish–American War – well before anticommunism became a favored bogeyman to justify forced regime change – the USA intervened in such countries as Nicaragua (and not so covertly either at that early stage, when norms of self-determination were still not strong) to implant favored rulers. Following World War II, the CIA tried out its regime change strategy far away from its backyard, in Iran. This strategy was then more or less replicated in Guatemala, and practiced intermittently across a number of client states, with the eventual overthrow of Allende in Chile being the most notorious of such cases.

Finally, the USA has collaborated with other imperial powers to pursue its economic interests in the Global South. Collaboration among imperialists is hardly new; Britain and France worked together in countries like Egypt to collect debt; and then, of course, a number of European powers decided to carve up Africa among themselves in the late nineteenth century. A commitment to antiimperialism notwithstanding, the USA was already participating in such discussions in the nineteenth century; for example, it participated in – and was a signatory to – the Berlin Conference in 1885 that laid the foundation for the Scramble for Africa. The first substantive major American move in this direction then came following the Spanish–American War, when the USA called upon all imperialist powers to agree to keep China stable and economically open for all to exploit. This well-known Open-Door policy arguably cast the dye for another American approach to establishing global influence: multilateral collaboration (Williams, 1962). Following World War II, American efforts to establish an open global economic order, supported by such multilateral institutions as the World Bank and the IMF – with a lead role for the Americans within these institutions – can certainly be interpreted as examples of a latter-day Open-Door policy. Much more pertinent for our purposes were the American efforts during the 1980s and the 1990s to use the World Bank and the IMF to ensure that developing countries paid off their foreign debts, especially the debt owed by large Latin American countries to American banks.

Multilateral collaboration as a strategy for building an informal empire served several American purposes. With an enormous power surplus and a competitive economy, the USA really did not need to control peripheral territories. If the USA could get other industrial powers to agree to keep the Global South open for all, then conflict among such powers could be reduced. Moreover, in a world in which state sovereignty had become a valued norm, the pursuit of American economic interests via such multilateral institutions as the World Bank or the IMF provided a fig leaf for American imperial ambitions. These institutions pushed pro-American ideologies of development as mere technical solutions to problems of development. Similarly, an effort to roll back the state in the developing world to ensure economic openness, especially in Latin America and Africa, could be packaged as a "bitter pill" that would ensure long-term health. And finally, unlike bilateral interventions – via open warfare or covert regime change – multilateral interventions seem especially well suited when the imperial goals involve pressuring a group of peripheral countries to follow a desired path.

3.3 British versus American Pathways to Empire

While the core focus of this Element is on the shared traits – the causes and the consequences – of British and American imperialism, it is also important to note a fairly obvious but important point: British and American approaches to empire-building varied quite a bit. Some of the differences were in part a function of the fact that Britain and the USA were different types of political economies but also because they came to empire-building more than a century apart, a time period during which the global context of imperialism changed sharply. Compared to industrializing Britain, for example, American corporations had access to a continent-sized economy at home. In this important sense, the USA was relatively self-sufficient. Like Britain, the USA also sought markets abroad from the late nineteenth century onward, but the urgency was never the same. Britain needed an empire to sustain its industrial drive; the USA merely wanted one. As a result, imperialism for Americans has always been more a matter of choice. The political class in Britain seldom questioned the merits of an empire. By contrast, Americans have always approached global expansionism with a degree of tentativeness, manifest in recurring debates about the merits of intervening in one place or another.

A continent-sized economy also provided a base on which Americans built a giant military-industrial complex. Compared to Britain in the nineteenth century, the USA has thus been a lot more powerful than its nearest competitor during the post–World War II period. Tight power competition had forced the British to be relatively "efficient" imperialists, especially in the sense that the British often made the imperialized pay for the privilege of being ruled by Britain. By contrast, power surplus has enabled Americans to pursue some imperial adventures – especially military adventures – without regards to their cost-effectiveness, even encouraging them to indulge their ideological whims. This was certainly the case in Vietnam, especially as the war dragged on. Even when it was clear that the USA was not likely to prevail over North Vietnam, American decision-makers continued to pursue an expensive and tragic war for the sake of prestige and credibility. A period of remorse followed. However, the remorse did not last long. The USA readily absorbed the costs and again moved on to a next set of imperial follies, most recently in Iraq and Afghanistan. Only time will tell whether there is a learning curve among American decision-makers, or instead, the past will be forgotten again, and another "forever war" will recommence.

The emergence of mass politics in the twentieth century has further created new challenges for American imperialism. Public opinion was not a huge factor in the making of the British Empire in so far as Britain's ruling class in the nineteenth century was relatively narrow. While public opinion is seldom decisive, even in the making of US foreign policy in the post–World War II period, it can become a significant constraint, as was evident during American intervention in Vietnam. The constraints thrown up by mass politics are even more evident in how politics came to be organized in peripheral countries following World War II. The emergence of postcolonial nationalism and states in these countries, for example, altered the challenges for any would-be imperialist. Over the last decades then, it is not surprising that the USA has often sought covert means to seek compliance in one country or another, hoping to avoid nationalist opposition to its imperial quests.

Emergence of mass politics has especially made the prospect of finding ready collaborators on the periphery difficult. Recall that British imperial arrangements often rested on the backs of ready collaborators in peripheral countries who could control and pacify the local population. During the second half of the twentieth century, spread of commerce and plebiscitarian politics altered the social structures of peripheral countries. Gone are the maharajas, the sultans, tribal chiefs, latifundistas, and the pashas of the past who collaborated with European imperialists. These intermediaries provided key building blocks of nineteenth-century imperialism. They are simply missing in the late twentieth century. The new collaborators of the twentieth century, say, military leaders or businessmen in the periphery, seldom enjoy mass following. As a result, imposing imperial order from the outside is considerably more challenging. American efforts to impose their order on others is thus often challenged by mobilized mass politics. Nationalism in peripheral countries has emerged as a powerful antidote to old-fashioned imperialism. It is thus not surprising that American attempts to establish informal empire works best – from an American point of view, that is – when it is pursued either via covert means or through multilateral institutions; by contrast, overt military interventions, such as in Vietnam, Iraq, and Afghanistan, are readily derailed by developing country nationalists.

4 The Impact of Imperialism

Imperialism has repeatedly retarded economic progress in the global periphery. This is true for both formal and informal empire, but to different degrees. The impact of colonialism – of formal empire – in shaping peripheral political economies was especially pernicious. This is because colonizing powers controlled the governments of their colonies. Without sovereign power, colonial economies were at the mercy of policy decisions made by self-interested metropolitan elite. Over time, these decisions turned most colonies into exporters of low-value-added commodities and importers of manufactured goods. Colonial economies experienced hardly any industrialization and very little economic growth. In the following discussion, the cases of British colonialism in India and Nigeria, and that of the USA in the Philippines support such an argument, while the case of industrialization in the Japanese colony of Korea helps underline the exceptional nature of such an outcome. Countries within the orbit of informal empire – informal colonies – experienced a little more economic progress than formal colonies, but not that much, and not all of them. Client rulers of some informal colonies enjoyed a semblance of political autonomy that they leveraged into commodity-led growth. Such growth, however, often followed a boom-and-bust pattern, reacting to global economic conditions; moreover, as in the case of formal colonies, informal colonies also experienced very little industrialization. The examples of Argentina, Brazil, and Egypt under British influence in the nineteenth century followed this pattern, as did such post–World War II American client states as Iran under the Shah and Chile under Pinochet. Once again, however, the case of South Korea under American tutelage helps qualify this discussion.

Better growth notwithstanding, the longer-term institutional legacy of informal empire may have been even more pernicious than that of colonialism. This is because nationalists in some colonies, especially in Asia, ruptured old colonial patterns in the post–World War II period, established sovereign and effective states, and put their countries on a forward path. By contrast, entrenched oligarchs in partially sovereign countries, say, in Latin America, helped sustain dependent political economies, first during the nineteenth century, and again in the post–World War II period. In recent decades then, especially during the heyday of the Washington Consensus, it was notable that select Asian countries – such as China, India, and Vietnam – used sovereign state power to put their respective countries on the path of broad-based development, including industrialization and rapid economic growth; by contrast, Latin American countries remained as highly unequal commodity exporters, heavily dependent on global economic conditions for their well-being.

The argument that imperialism retards economic progress on the global periphery is hardly novel. Many left-of-center and nationalist critics of imperialism, including scholars in the dependency tradition, have put forward similar claims in the past. However, there are two important reasons to revisit – and reformulate – these older claims. *First*, the nationalist generation in Asia and Africa has faded, as has much of dependency theory in Latin America.

The criticisms of colonialism and of neocolonialism are so forgotten that some observers now claim, with impunity, that, on balance, the impact of British colonialism, or of America's informal empire, was essentially benign (Gaddis, 1997; Ferguson, 2003). Evidence does not support such views. *Second*, and more important, unlike some Marxist and dependency critics of imperialism, I do not attribute the negative consequences of imperialism to global spread of capitalism. Of course, how the developing world came to be integrated into the global capitalist economy hurt their economic prospects. But there was nothing inevitable about these outcomes; much depended on the terms of global integration, terms that were set by more or less sovereign states. Japan escaped imperialism and used sovereign state power to industrialize in the nineteenth century. Countries with some sovereignty could – at least on occasion, such as in Argentina – leverage this autonomy into economic performance that was better than in full colonies during the nineteenth century. Client status notwithstanding, countries that were hived off from larger wholes like South Korea and Taiwan also used the state structures they inherited from Japanese colonialism to industrialize in the post–World War II period. In late twentieth century too, countries as diverse as China and India consolidated sovereign states and used that power to facilitate economic progress in the new millennium. By contrast, many African countries failed to translate formal sovereignty into effective state power, with poor economic performance the result. And many Latin American countries continued in the groove of dependent development, with middling economic performance. Clearly, more or less sovereign state power was a key variable linking imperialism to underdevelopment, not some inchoate force of global capitalism. In what follows then, I not only document the negative developmental impact of imperialism but clarify the underlying mechanisms; the argument is that, not capitalism alone, but sovereign and effective state power – that mediates the national impact of global capitalism – is what helps us understand the inverse relationship between imperialism and prospects of economic progress in the global periphery.

4.1 Impact of Colonialism

The history of colonialism is vast. A few caveats are thus in order. My comments here are limited to British and American colonialism, with a nod to the Japanese experience in Korea. Readers should keep in mind that even these limited observations leave out a lot: I do not focus here on Britain's white settlements say, in Australia, or on settler colonialism, such as in South Africa. I exemplify the discussion of the impact of British colonialism in Asia and Africa with reference to the cases of India and Nigeria, and that of American colonialism with reference to the Philippines. A focus on these cases again leaves out other cases. Also, the discussion here is relatively abbreviated, drawing on my own detailed studies elsewhere (Kohli, 2004, 2020).

Two centuries of British rule in India left behind a profoundly undeveloped economy but some functioning political institutions. The negative economic impact of prolonged British rule in India was transmitted via a variety of channels, including: squeezing India's economic resources but not investing them in areas that might benefit Indians; forced economic opening to ensure that India imported British manufactured goods and sold commodities abroad; and British foreign investments in India that were guaranteed a rate of return by the colonial state. Starting with the East India Company, and then continuing with Crown rule, the British taxed India at a very high rate. Much of this taxation originated in the countryside, where most Indians lived and worked. The total revenues collected by the British in India averaged 18–20 percent of the GDP of Indian territory under British control in the nineteenth century; nearly 60 percent of these revenues in turn came from taxing agricultural production. Taxing India's poor economy at such a high rate – year in and year out, decade after decade, for more than a century – obviously hurt the well-being of Indians, mostly poor peasants. More tragic were two other consequences. *First*, in order to collect land revenues, the British devised a variety of mechanisms, including assigning private property rights to mega-landowners and then holding them responsible for transmitting the revenues. Many landowners in turn parceled out land to tax collectors, building layers of parasitic classes that lived off the wealth of poor peasants. This pattern of land ownership created disincentives for all and sundry to invest in land, contributing to long-term stagnation in agricultural productivity. And *second*, much of the revenues that the British collected were used in a manner that did not benefit poor Indians. For example, very little was invested in improving, say, irrigation to help Indian agriculture become less monsoon-dependent; as noted in Section 2, nearly two-thirds of the revenues that the British collected went into covering the cost of the Indian empire, the bulk of which funded nothing else but the giant British Indian army.

If squeeze-and-neglect was the main mode of British exploitation of India in the early colonial period, forced opening of India facilitated the integration of Indian and British economies in the nineteenth century. British trade with India grew throughout the century. Without any political autonomy, Indians were in no position to shape the nature or the terms of this trade. Instead, Britain sold India manufactured goods, especially textiles, and imported raw materials in turn. As this trade progressed, India's substantial textile and other industries declined; for example, between 1801 and 1830, India's industrial output declined more than 30 percent (Broadberry et. al., 2015, table 11).

India's main export to Britain thus became raw cotton, but India always imported more from Britain than it exported. Britain, however, needed India to have a favorable balance of trade so as finance a variety of needs, such as to pay for British salaries and expenses in India, as well as to remit profits on growing foreign investments in the post-1857 period. This favorable balance was achieved by exporting Indian commodities to other parts of the world. Especially notable in this context was the sale of opium to China that flourished following the Opium Wars; by the mid-century, for example, nearly a third of India's total exports was opium. Under British tutelage then, India became a classic economic colony that imported manufactured goods in exchange for low-value-added commodities. When India finally developed some industry in the early twentieth century, it was in spite of – and not because of – British presence; among the underlying factors that facilitated this shift was de facto import substitution that emerged behind British tariffs in India that in turn were aimed at raising revenues, as well as keeping Japanese and German manufactured goods out of India.

Once Crown rule was established over India, British foreign investments in India also grew. The building of railroads that crisscrossed the subcontinent was thus a notable development of the second half of the twentieth century. Railroads enabled the British to access markets in the Indian interior as well as move troops in and around India. No wonder, the British state and private entrepreneurs collaborated closely in building Indian railroads. The British colonial state guaranteed a rate of return – around 5 percent – to British entrepreneurs who invested in spreading Britain's second industrial revolution to India. The hypocrisy of *laissez-faire* aside, these guarantees ensured significant movement of private capital to India. British companies used the capital to buy British goods needed – anywhere from rail lines to locomotives – to create a sprawling network of Indian railways. The British state further facilitated availability of land and labor in India. Whether the railways were a profitable investment or not really did not matter; a steady rate of return was guaranteed from the revenues that the British colonial state collected in India. And where did these revenues come from? Mostly from poor Indian peasants! Without political autonomy, Indians were in no position to alter these terms of foreign investment; Indian nationalists cried hoarse but in vain.[19] The cumulative economic impact of British colonial rule in India is evident in the fact that per capita incomes of Indians between, say, 1820 and 1950, barely budged

---

[19] As we will see later on, similar developments in other parts of the world evolved differently; for example, the British also built railroads in Brazil on similar exploitative terms but, with some political autonomy, Brazilians at the turn of the twentieth century nationalized British-owned railways. Indians had to wait another five decades before they could reverse such exploitative arrangements.

(Madison, 2007, table A 7); when the British left India after two centuries of rule, more than 80 percent of Indians were illiterate and the life expectancy of an average Indian was thirty-two years.

The longer-term political legacy of British colonial rule in India was somewhat more benign. For their own reasons, the British in India created and left behind a sizable army and a civil service. These professional bureaucracies came to constitute the heart of the sovereign Indian state, and served India well. As important, the British colonial state provided the framework for the emergence of a powerful nationalist movement in India. Educated Indians went for further training to Britain and came back demanding self-determination. Led by the likes of Mahatma Gandhi and Nehru, these demands grew into a relatively cohesive mass movement – represented by the Indian National Congress – that eventually pushed the British out of India. The fact that the autocratic colonial state was relatively centralized provided incentives for Indians from a variety of ethnic backgrounds to pull together; bickering only encouraged the British proclivity to divide-and-rule. While the religious divide between Hindus and Muslims proved difficult to bridge – difficulties that eventually created the separate states of India, Pakistan, and eventually Bangladesh, out of the British Indian colony – the Indian National Congress managed to generate a workable unity among India's diverse ethnic groups. Moreover, a successful nationalist movement also generated a measure of consensus among India's political class concerning the nature of the sovereign Indian state: self-reliant; democratic; and a federal republic. When grafted on top of a relatively well-functioning army and civil service, this civilian consensus in India facilitated the emergence of a moderately well-functioning democratic state. While Indian democracy was far from perfect – then or now – it is the case that, by developing-country standards, India emerged from colonialism with a set of institutions that have helped Indian leaders steer the profoundly underdeveloped economy of that country on a path of modernization.

As in the case of India, British colonialism in Nigeria left behind a commodity-exporting economy that imported British manufactured goods. Unlike India, however, what the British left behind in Nigeria's political sphere was a highly dysfunctional state. Nigeria entered a civil war within a few years of decolonization. A dysfunctional state, in turn, has repeatedly failed to translate formal sovereignty into an effective capacity to use Nigeria's considerable economic potential to good use. The long-term legacy of colonialism in Nigeria – as in many other African countries – has proven to be downright deleterious.

As noted earlier, British colonial goals in Nigeria were minimal: to keep the French out and to promote trade. The British thus chose to run Nigeria on the cheap, without expending much effort to either develop a state structure or promote economic change. A number of political developments in the first half of the twentieth century help us understand the colonial origins of the ineffective Nigerian state. *First*, after subduing Yoruba chiefs in the southwest and defeating the emirs of the northern Sokoto caliphate militarily, the British at the turn of the twentieth century decided to pursue the cost-effective ruling strategy of indirect rule. This led them into alliances with traditional and personalistic rulers of a variety of sorts in Nigeria. Unlike colonial India, very little effort went into creating a professional colonial army or a civil service. Under the British umbrella, colonial Nigeria thus came to be dotted by numerous "decentralized despots."[20] These traditional rulers treated their respective realms as personal fiefdoms. Nigeria thus never developed any clear boundaries between public and private realms, a distinction that is often a prerequisite for the establishment of a modern state. This fusion of the public and private spheres has in turn continued to plague the functioning of the Nigerian state, well into recent time periods.

A *second* related development was the failure of the British to centralize power in colonial Nigeria. The British created Nigeria but never really created a functioning central government. Nigeria was ruled instead as three regions, the northern region populated mainly by Hausa-Fulani, the southwest by the Yoruba, and the southeast by the Igbo. Early decisions in this direction stemmed from expedience; any effort to create an effective central government would have required not only creating a central army and civil service, but also renegotiating power-sharing arrangements with traditional rulers. With minimal colonial goals in mind, the British did not have any incentive to pursue these difficult political tasks. Repeated efforts in this direction then amounted to little. Over time, the divisions born of expediency hardened as an administrative grid created differing interests and identities around regions. The Islamic emirs of the north, for example, resisted Christian missionaries and English-language education that came with them. The British obliged their junior ruling partners and kept missionaries out of the north. As a result, northern Nigeria lagged behind in education; traditional rulers also eventually proved to be reluctant nationalists. By contrast, the southwest was more commercial, even from earlier slave-trading centuries. Missionary education introduced the English language. Many educated Yoruba then went to Britain to study and some came back as nationalists. Better educated, and with higher per capita incomes, the Yoruba under the British developed different interests and a different identity from the Islamic northerners. The Ibo also moved in their own direction, even demanding a separate country following independence, leading to the infamous Biafra War.

---

[20] This evocative concept is borrowed (though used a little differently) from Mamdani (1996).

A cohesive anticolonial nationalist movement in Nigeria might have over-come the fragmented authority structures that the British created and left behind. Unfortunately, this was not to be. Instead, Nigeria's nationalist move-ment came to mirror the fractures of the poorly designed colonial state. To begin with, the British were in Nigeria for only six decades. By the time the British left, the educated political class that might have sprouted would-be Nigerian nationalists was still pretty tiny. Worse, this political class was regionally fragmented, with Yoruba elite being the most educated and politically active. The power of northern emirs rested on British tutelage; they were thus suspi-cious of these "new men" of the south who demanded freedom from British colonialism. The two never really joined ranks, weakening the anticolonial impulse. Had the Nigerian colonial state been more cohesive to begin with, emerging nationalists would have had to overcome their differences to fight the British successfully. As it was, it proved to be more convenient for regional Nigerian elite to demand more resources for their respective regions. A fragmented nationalist movement thus came to be grafted atop a poorly constructed colonial state, eventually pulling sovereign Nigeria in different directions. The fact that many among the Nigerian elite treated politics as an extension of their private interests – with a weak sense of public purpose – only added to political woes. Unlike India then, the British in Nigeria left behind a fragmented polity infused with personalism, a set of traits that did not serve Nigeria well in the future.

On the economic front, the main British interest in Nigeria was trade. Over time, Nigeria became a classic colonial economy that exported commodities – palm oil, groundnuts, cocoa, cotton, and tin – and took in such manufactured goods as textiles, alcohol, and metal products. The British also taxed this trade as a major source of revenues that helped run the colonial state. Little of these revenues were spent on improving agriculture, the main stay of the Nigerian economy. What little was spent to improve agricultural production went on exportable cash crops, and the resulting growth was mainly exten-sive, with little improvement in productivity. As a result, subsistence agricul-ture dominated Nigeria's economy for the colonial period, with little improvement over the six decades. As to industry, the impulse was weak. What there was, the British actively discouraged. Some foreign investment helped start an industry here or there – a soap factory, cigarette manufacturing, a handful of sawmills and cotton gins – but for the most part, British interest in Nigeria was to sell their manufactured products rather than export capital. Following World War II, there was some commodity-led growth, especially during the Korean War, though this growth too followed the well-understood pattern of boom and bust. In sum, the overall economic impact of British rule in

Nigeria was negligible economic progress: When the British came to Nigeria, the hand hoe was the main instrument of production in the countryside; when the British left, the hand hoe was still the main tool used for cultivation in the fields.

During the same time period that the British ran Nigeria as a colony, the Americans too tried their hand at colonialism in the Philippines. American motives and interests have already been discussed. As to impact, it is important to keep in mind that Americans in the Philippines inherited a territory that had long been a Spanish colony – the roots of all that has gone wrong in the Philippines thus has a long past and the blame needs to be shared. Nevertheless, the evidence does not support the self-serving claims of American exceptionalism: over time, the colonial state that the Americans created turned into an ineffective state, and the economy of the Philippines under American rule evolved along standard colonial lines, exporting commodities in exchange for manufactured goods. The American ruling strategy in the Philippines sought to repress Filipino nationalists on the one hand and to coopt those willing to cooperate on the other hand. Indigenous landed oligarchs became a key ally of the Americans. Members of urban middle classes could have posed a serious nationalist challenge but they were skillfully coopted into a state structure that offered them little real power – that remained in the hands of the Americans – but plenty of opportunity for graft and gain. The colonial ruling arrangement in the Philippines was thus profoundly hypocritical: For five decades, Americans talked about independence while running a colony, and the Filipino elite also talked about independence while cooperating with the Americans. Most Filipinos were of course left out of this convenient colonial alliance.

Following their own ideals, Americans introduced elements of democracy in the Philippines, including elections, legislature, rule of law, and a free press. On this dimension, the American legacy was more positive than that of many other colonizers. American rule in the Philippines was definitely less brutal than, say, that of the Japanese in neighboring Korea (more on that later). However, judged from the standpoint of a longer-term political legacy, Americans helped create a fairly ineffective state, so much so that the Philippines in the second half of the twentieth century remained an exception to the state-led economic boom in much of East Asia. This is because the Americans put hardly any effort into creating a professional bureaucracy in the Philippines. American focus instead was on elections and parties. Since American colonial strategy had empowered agrarian oligarchs and urban middle classes, members of these groups penetrated these institutions and used them for self-aggrandizement. The colonial state was thus both hollow and corrupt – hollow in the sense that real power lay beyond the state, in the hands of the Americans and, without a rational bureau-cracy, it evolved into a state without capacity to get things done; and corrupt because limited public resources were channeled into private uses, contributing to the long-term making of an ineffective, neopatrimonial state.

As noted earlier, the USA did not acquire the Philippines with economic motives in mind; the Philippines was instead to serve as America's Hong Kong, a stepping stone to the lucrative China market. Once acquired, however, the USA did turn the Philippine economy into a colonial economy that served American interests. As in British cases, Americans decided early that colonial rule in the Philippines will be financed by Filipino resources; American rhetoric of "helping" their "brown brothers" aside, there was nothing philanthropic about American colonial rule. Americans collected these resources mainly by imposing a regressive flat tax on the Filipinos, an arrangement that the collab-orating Filipino elite could support. Most of these resources went toward running the colonial state. To be fair, what little was left, the Americans made good use of public resources by investing them into education and health. What the Filipinos learned in the classroom was, however, deeply controlled to stifle any indigenous nationalist sentiments. Colonial education was thus a double-edged sword: It promoted literacy but it was also used as a propaganda tool by the colonizers.

Sugar exports from the Philippines to the USA grew sharply in the early colonial decades. Americans also invested some public resources into irrigation during the 1910s. As a result, the Filipino economy grew during the first two decades of American colonial rule. During this period there were also the beginnings of some simple manufacturing within the Philippines. Most of these early positive trends came to an end, due to the following underlying changes. *First*, as a result of legal changes in the USA (the legal decisions concerning the so-called insular cases), the colonial state in the Philippines was unable to tax trade with the USA. Public revenues within the Philippines thus declined, with a negative impact on public investments in irrigation and agri-cultural production. *Second*, sugar lobbyists within the USA succeeded in limiting tariff-free sugar exports from the Philippines to the USA. While sugar exports from the Philippines still grew, tariffs did discourage economic growth. By contrast, manufacturing interests in the USA succeeded in pushing legislation that enabled tariff-free exports to the Philippines. What little manu-facturing had begun in the Philippines was thus destroyed. *Third*, the great depression of the 1930s did not help. And *fourth*, American foreign investment in mining grew, mainly as a pathway to export minerals back to the USA. Over the five decades of American colonial rule then, the Filipino economy became another classic colonial economy that exported commodities to the metropole and imported their manufactured goods. There was some economic growth in the early decades, especially when sugarcane production was supported by public investments in irrigation but this too decelerated. There is nothing really surprising about these developments except that they do fly in the face of Americans forgetting – or denying – their imperial past. Doubly unfortunate for the Philippines, the colonial state that the Americans helped construct eventually proved to be ineffective in reversing the colonial economic patterns during the second half of the twentieth century.

Such colonies as India, Nigeria, and the Philippines then became integrated with metropolitan economies – Britain and the USA – as takers of manufactured goods and exporters of low-value-added commodities. The main political legacy of colonialism was in turn to create the framework of a modern state in these peripheral societies but to also strengthen the hands of personalistic indigenous elite. One exception to these general economic and political legacies of colonialism was Japanese rule in Korea. In so far as exceptions help to prove a rule, a brief discussion of this case might be useful at this point. While the Japanese too were driven to imperialism in search of economic and political opportunities, how Japan ruled its colonies had some unique features. Japan was a late modernizer. The Meiji model of development took inspiration from the Prussians. The Japanese then prioritized the construction of a rational-legal bureaucracy at the heart of an autocratic, modernizing state at home, as well as in its colonies, such as in Korea. Japan also colonized countries with which it shared racial and cultural links. It was easy for Meiji oligarchs to imagine that, over time, Korea and Taiwan could be permanently incorporated into a Japanese empire. This hope – if not quite a plan – was consequential in terms of imperial policies in such areas as industrialization and education. And finally, a country like Korea was just across a narrow strait of water from Japan; the situation was more akin to Britain in Ireland, than to Britain in India or the USA in the Philippines. Moreover, Japan had pried Korea away from China, and Russia too had ambitions in Korea. The Japanese Empire in Korea was thus highly militarized. Numerous Japanese bureaucrats also moved across the narrow straits to help rule Korea, and Japanese companies and individuals came to own substantial amount of agricultural land in Korea.

Japanese rule in Korea was ruthless, probably more so than British and American rule in many of their colonies. Japan also exploited Korean economic resources for its own benefit. On this dimension at least, colonialism seems to have an undifferentiated history. And yet, some of the unique features of Japanese colonialism – late modernizer, with a focus on state-led development; colonizing neighbors with cultural and racial similarities; and enormous physical presence across a narrow strait – bequeathed legacies that too were somewhat unique in the history of colonialism; these need underlining. First, the Japanese created and left behind an efficacious state in Korea. Following their own model, Meiji oligarchs in Korea pensioned off Korean landlord classes from state offices and replaced them with a professional bureaucracy. The results were evident in short order. For example, prior to colonial rule, Korean leaders had tried in vain to undertake a cadastral survey so as to enhance state revenues. These efforts were often frustrated by state officials with roots in landed wealth. Once pensioned off, the new colonial state was now in a position to undertake tasks in the countryside. Colonial officials then carried out a successful survey of land ownership rights. The aim was of course enlarging the tax base to finance colonial rule; during the process, however, the Japanese also started creating a state in Korea that was less neopatrimonial and more adept at getting things done. Over the next few decades, the Japanese in Korea experimented with how to develop a state structure that would respond to central directives; this experimentation included higher salaries, punishment for corruption, and strict professionalization and socialization. As new tasks emerged – of course, most of them aimed at benefitting the Japanese – the colonial state in Korea proved to be relatively efficacious, with long-term consequences.

During the 1920s, the Japanese used the newly restructured colonial state in Korea to improve rice production in Korea. The colonial state used lower-level bureaucrats to spread better agricultural practices, leading to gains in product-ivity in the countryside. The aim of such policies was of course not to benefit the Koreans but to feed the growing Japanese working class at home. Nevertheless, longer-term legacies included a state that could penetrate downward, as well as higher rice yields per unit of land. The contrast with Britain in Nigeria during the same period is striking; the British in Nigeria neither created a functioning state nor facilitated any changes in agricultural production. It is not that the Japanese were better imperialists. No. The differences instead were driven by circumstances: The Japanese ate rice just like the Koreans; they could use the efficacious colonial state to transmit better production techniques; and then they could readily transport Korean rice cheaply across a narrow strait of water to feed their own citizens.

Similarly, the Japanese helped initiate industry in Korea. This too is relatively unique in the history of colonialism. Several factors help us understand these developments. The Japanese hoped to incorporate Korea permanently. That is why they coerced the Koreans to learn Japanese and to adopt Japanese names. As part of the same long-term project – which of course crashed in Hiroshima and Nagasaki – building industry in its colonies was not as much of a contradiction for the Japanese as it might have been for the British in India or for the USA in the Philippines. The British and the Americans mainly wanted to sell manufactured goods to their colonies; for them, establishing manufacturing plants in the colonies would have undermined their exporting interests. The Japanese also faced these pulls and pushes. However, active involvement of the state in the economy enabled them to work through some of these tensions. Japanese leaders worked closely with zaibatsu (big business houses), helping promote exports of some, and cajoling yet others to start new industries in Korea. What gave urgency to Japanese industrialization initiatives in Korea were war-related aims in China; heavy industry on the mainland provided distinct strategic advantages. Military and commercial aims then combined, leading to the beginnings of industry in Korea under Japanese auspices. By 1940 then, agriculture and industry contributed nearly the same share to the Korean national product, a remarkable figure for a colony.

Finally, as the Japanese transferred their own state-led model of late industrialization to Korea, they also transferred such practices as labor control. Interwar Japan was an autocratic, militarized political economy. Labor in Japan was tightly controlled from above. As Korea began its industrialization during the colonial period, repressive control of labor in the interests of production also became an integral part of the Korean political economy. A sovereign Korea then came to inherit key elements of the Japanese model of development: an effective developmental state; close cooperation between the state and big business houses to promote industry; and tightly controlled labor. While far from liberal, these key political and economic attributes served South Korea well as it undertook rapid industrialization during the 1970s. As I will argue later, the Korean "economic miracle" under Park Chung Hee is best understood as building on this somewhat unique colonial legacy of Japanese colonialism; moreover, South Korea succeeded in spite of being an American client state, not because of it.

To sum up the discussion, for the most part, metropolitan powers shaped their colonies as exporters of commodities and importers of manufactured goods. Even commodity-based economic growth was rare and intermittent. This much was evident from a discussion of India, Nigeria, and the Philippines. A brief look back at the case of Japan in Korea underlines how rare the cases of industrial growth under colonial auspices really were. Following decolonization, the capacity of developing countries to steer economic development depended on the nature of the state that they inherited or created anew. Once again, the beginnings of a more rational-legal developmental state in Korea stands out as an exception. The more general political legacy of colonialism was instead to strengthen the hands of the premodern indigenous elite, who in turn bequeathed a patrimonial tendency to colonially constructed state structures.

Strong nationalist movements – led by the urban elite – altered these patterns in a few places, such as India, but for the most part, such as in sub-Saharan Africa, colonialism left behind personalistic and ill-formed states that were incapable of promoting sustained economic development.

4.2 Impact of Informal Empire

Colonialism has faded. Informal empire continues. It is thus important to understand the typical impact of informal modes of control that metropolitan powers exercise over select peripheral economies. A discussion of Britain's informal empire in Argentina, Egypt, and China in the nineteenth century is followed here by how the USA shaped some such countries in the second half of the twentieth century as Iran, Chile, and South Korea. When compared to the impact of colonialism, the main pattern that emerges is of lop-sided development:[21] a little better economic growth but the empowerment of a ruling elite who prefer a dependent rather than a nationalist path to development.

Britain's informal empire in Argentina lasted nearly a full century, say, from the early nineteenth to the early twentieth century. During this century, the Argentine economy experienced considerable growth: per capita income grew at some 0.8 percent per annum during 1820 and 1870 and then even more rapidly from 1870 to World War I. At the turn of the twentieth century, Buenos Aires rivaled New York City for its opulence. Unfortunately, the underlying economies were very different. Much of Argentina's growth was propelled by low-value-added exports – especially products of a ranch-based economy – to Britain and elsewhere. This economy failed to diversify; there was very little industrialization. Instead, Argentina continued to import manufactured goods from Britain, textiles in the first half of the nineteenth century, and then railways and other heavier industrial products in the second half of the century. Eventually, Argentina paid a heavy cost in the twentieth century for this easy development in the nineteenth century. Following the depression of the 1930s, for example, the Argentine economy never recovered its past glory. Since then, it has struggled under a variety of governments to create balanced and equitable growth, but in vain. Today, Argentina remains one of the more troubled economies of the world.

The context of an informal empire helps us understand both the early growth and the subsequent economic problems of Argentina. The Argentine and British economies proved to be highly complementary in the nineteenth century: A land abundant country, Argentina provided products of a ranch-based economy to

---

[21] The term, "lop-sided development," is borrowed from Issawi (1961).

Britain for much of the century and, in turn, absorbed British manufactured goods. Since Argentina was a formally sovereign country – though constrained – most of these economic interactions occurred on commercial terms, helping the profitability of Argentine producers. In addition, Britain provided loans – often on usurious terms – and helped build infrastructure and public utilities in Argentina. With imported luxuries, the Argentine elite could nearly believe in the nineteenth century that they were living in a rapidly modernizing country. What sustained these economic patterns was a ruling coalition of ranchers and merchants in Argentina that the British helped install and nurtured. Since these ruling elite benefitted handsomely from Argentina's commodity-led growth under British tutelage, they repeatedly ignored the longer-term interests of the country: The economy grew without much capital accumulation; inequalities grew sharply; and there was little investment in building human capital or technical skills. On occasion, there were demands to pursue more of a "national project," something akin to what was happening in the USA at the time, namely, deliberate industrialization. The Argentine ruling class, however, had little interest or inclination in pursuing this path; they identified more with fellow Europeans elsewhere than with the masses they ruled. The British also sided with this ruling class to ensure that the more nationalist elements within it did not rise to power; they helped ensure that the national polity in Argentina served the interests of ranchers first and thus ensured that the architecture of an informal empire endured.

As Britain's global power declined in the early twentieth century, the old governing patterns within Argentina came unstuck. Wars and depression then disrupted the trade patterns on which the nineteenth-century Argentine growth rested. American power in Latin America was growing but the USA was itself a giant agricultural economy; American interests in a country like Argentina were rather different than that of Britain. The USA too wanted access to markets in Latin America in the post–World War II period but not for the sake of their agricultural products. The power of agrarian oligarchs in Argentina then declined. As populist leaders emerged, they found ready supporters among those that the commodity-exporting economy had failed to benefit. However, populist leaders hardly had an effective program for industrialization. Indigenous capitalists were too small to take a lead and the state hardly encouraged them to grow. Weak national capitalism was and remains the Achilles' heel for many Latin American countries like Argentina. The core development program focused instead on import substituting industrialization (ISI) led by foreign investors. This turned out to be a poor substitute for a real transformation of a national economy. Populists like Juan Perón then promised the moon to everyone, without delivering much.

The antiimperialist rhetoric of populists also threatened American interests in the hemisphere, especially in the context of the emerging Cold War. In search of collaborators, the USA trained militaries in countries like Argentina. The military elite in turn forged coalitions with declining agrarian oligarchs and foreign investors who might still facilitate prosperity for the elite. But it was too late in history for such easy developmental pathways. There were limits to how much demand elite incomes alone could generate; without income distribution, ISI was not sustainable. With relatively higher incomes and wages, export promotion was also not easy. Stuck between a rock and a hard place, countries like Argentina continued to look for an easy way out. Debt-led growth during the 1970s and beyond then provided yet another episode in the drama of recurring developmental failures; I will return to a discussion of how countries like Argentina fared under the Washington Consensus of the late twentieth century.

The impact of Britain's informal empire on Egypt provides another important case of how during the nineteenth century Britain repeatedly turned peripheral economies into commodity exporters for its own advantage. What is so dramatic about the Egyptian case is that Britain deliberately destroyed the modernizing efforts underway in that country at the beginning of the century. As noted earlier, Mohammed Ali sought to modernize the Egyptian state and economy. As these efforts started to bear fruit, they threatened the Ottomans and challenged Britain's interests in the region. The British then used their superior power to impose a number of restrictions on Egypt that undermined both its industry and military. Within the framework of an informal empire, the British encouraged the production of raw cotton in Egypt to be used for textile manufacturing back home and, in turn, sold textiles and other manufactured goods to Egypt. During the second half of the nineteenth century, Britain also exported materials needed to build railways across Egypt. Egyptian rulers often borrowed money from Britain (and France) to pursue a variety of infrastructure projects, including the building of the Suez Canal. Similar to elsewhere during the second half of the nineteenth century, Egypt became a heavily indebted country. Using debt as leverage, Britain and France became directly involved in running the Egyptian state, especially areas that had a bearing on Egypt's capacity to pay back its debts. Such overt involvement of foreigners in matters political provoked indigenous nationalist response, aimed both at the foreigners and at the khedives who collaborated with European powers. The British then intervened militarily in 1882 to crush these nationalists and turned Egypt into a near-colony. Even though Egypt became formally sovereign in 1922, its political autonomy remained pretty restricted till the nationalist coup led by Nasser in 1952.

During the long nineteenth century then, Britain turned Egypt into a classic colonial economy: a large, foreign-controlled cotton plantation of sorts (with the pyramids and the Nile), which attracted investment to support cotton production, sold its cotton to Britain, and bought British-manufactured cotton goods in return. The British also introduced private property to Egypt, helping prop up an upper class that collaborated with foreigners. As in the case of Argentina, the Egyptian economy grew for much of the century. The main source of this growth was cotton exports, fueled by investment in irrigation. Mohammed Ali had initiated such investments in the early part of the century. In one form or another, Mohammed Ali's successors maintained these public investments, supporting growth of cotton exports and thus of the overall economy; after all, these exports were the main source of growth in elite incomes. That a measure of political autonomy was essential for supporting this growth is also sharply underscored by the Egyptian case. As Britain's grip on Egypt tightened, British proconsuls channeled public resources away from investment in irrigation to debt repayments. With this decline, economic growth in Egypt first decelerated during the last two decades of the twentieth century. This was still good in comparison to what followed: In the new century, per capita agricultural output in Egypt declined steadily until World War I, and then did not climb back to its late nineteenth century levels until the 1960s.

In addition to the core trading and financial relations, the movement of British and other foreigners to Egypt, a dearth of higher education, and the pattern of foreign investments were the other important economic developments during the long imperial era. With the British ensuring property and security during the second half of the nineteenth century, large number of foreigners moved into port cities like Alexandria, but also Cairo. Imperial laws freed these foreigners from local taxation laws; this in turn further hurt the financial health of the Egyptian state. These foreigners often filled economic niches that an emerging indigenous middle class might have filled in a commodity-exporting economy, forestalling the development of such a class. Britain's education policy in Egypt had a similar impact. Wary of educated nationalists – a lesson learnt from India – the British in Egypt did not introduce higher education. This then further contributed to the dearth of a commercial and professional middle class, leaving a vacuum of sorts in the middle of the class structure that eventually hurt prospects of democracy and empowered military officers to be representatives of Egyptian nationalism. Moreover, foreign investment under British tutelage moved into areas deeply connected to the cotton-exporting economy: mortgage companies; banking; and some infrastructure development. None of this contributed to the diversification of the Egyptian economy in any significant way. When one Egyptian ruler or another sought to support some indigenous manufacturing, the British actively discouraged such moves by imposing onerous taxes. During the years of the depression and World War II, as trade was disrupted, some de facto industrialization occurred. Real efforts to promote an industrial economy did not commence until the British were thrown out of Egypt in the 1950s – by Nasser, a military officer – more than a century after Mohammed Ali's efforts in that direction were thwarted by the British.

Britain's informal empire in China was bookended by the Opium Wars and World War I. Over those six to seven decades, the Chinese economy pretty well stagnated, and the Chinese state disintegrated. The British impact on China has to be understood within this context: While China was coming apart due to its own internal tensions, British interventions made matters worse for China. The main vectors along which the British impact on China unfolded were not always the same as in Argentina or Egypt. For one thing, Britain's economic presence in China was relatively limited. China never became a dependent economy in the sense of becoming a producer of a few commodities linked to the growth of international trade. Of course, China exported tea but China was a giant economy; exports from China averaged only 3–4 percent of China's gross national product. The steady growth of tea exports from China thus neither lifted Chinese economic growth over the century nor displaced food-crop production in any big way. Much of Chinese agriculture continued to cater to China's huge agrarian population. The British also did not own agricultural land in China. China's landowning classes never became champions of free trade, which would have made them allied with the British. Imperial incursions in China were thus mainly urban, what one specialist described as numerous "micro-colonies" along the coast and the Yangtze river (Osterhammel, 1999). The overall impact of such urban incursions was not dramatic.

The much more significant – and pernicious – areas of British interventions in China were the opium trade and limiting the autonomy of the Chinese state. As to the opium trade, nearly one out of every ten Chinese people had become an opium addict by the end of the nineteenth century. Britain was strongly implicated in this development. Britain opened China at gunpoint in the name of free trade and then used that opening to push opium produced in British India. The opium that was cultivated in India was deliberately designed to meet Chinese tastes and needs. How did opium addiction on a large-scale impact China's capacity for governance and economic development? Though causal connections are hard to specify, we can be sure that the results were negative, maybe even sharply negative. If one is not persuaded, think of a modern-day health situation, such as the spread of HIV. If one out of every ten citizens of any country become infected with HIV, it is considered a crisis that demands global attention. To make matters worse, opium addiction in China was concentrated among working-age men; nearly half of Chinese working men might have been addicts. How could this not have had a deleterious impact on the society? The British forced opium into China for the sake of profits. Nothing then underscores the hypocrisy of nineteenth-century British liberalism more sharply than the opium trade.

And finally, Britain's more direct political impact on China should be underscored. Britain's informal empire rested on undermining the efficacy of the Chinese state; its political autonomy had to be undermined for the British to pursue their economic interests. This they did systematically and brutally. Wars led to treaties that reduced tariffs and duties, sources that may have augmented the resource base of the Chinese state. The British came to control the use of custom duties, significant portions of which went to pay indemnities. And tariffs as a policy option were not available to Chinese rulers, making it difficult to encourage domestic industry later in the century when the Empress Dowager initiated the self-strengthening movement. Resource constraints made it difficult to build armed forces and to impose order on rebellious groups. The more dependent the Chinese state became on warlords below and the British above, the more the state lost its legitimacy. The Empress Dowager tried to save her power and the monarchial state by joining forces with the Boxers. A decisive defeat at the hands of foreign power then put the last nails in the coffin of the Chinese state. Unlike Meiji restoration in neighboring Japan, the Chinese state in the nineteenth century proved incapable of initiating modernization. Britain's informal empire over nineteenth-century China thus reinforced domestic trends within China to ensure that there would be no Meiji-like restoration in China.

Britain's informal empire cast a long shadow on the client states within its orbit, a shadow not as dark as in cases of colonialism, but a shadow nevertheless. The three examples discussed here in brief underline that in each case, the British actively discouraged – and succeeded – in forestalling the emergence of nationalistic rulers and industrial economies. Over the nineteenth century, the growth impact varied, from considerable growth in Argentina to near stagnation in China. The Egyptian case is especially telling in so far as it points to the underlying dynamics: The Egyptian economy grew for several decades but then economic growth declined toward the end of the century as British grip over Egypt tightened, turning it into more of a colony. The political impact varied too. The Argentine elite benefitted from strong economic ties with Britain and remained a powerful force that favored a dependent economy well into the twentieth century; as we will see later, the USA found ready partners with remnants of this elite again toward the end of the twentieth century. By contrast, nationalists in both Egypt and China sought to break the imperial yoke following World War II, with Mao a lot more successful than Nasser.

The impact of American interventions in the post–World War II period also moved in a similar direction. The USA repeatedly sought to undermine nationalists in countries that mattered to it and instead to promote leaders that favored a client status with an open economy. Though the USA did not always succeed, the pattern of interventions was similar. During the Cold War, an incomplete list of major American interventions – either to support or to oppose emerging political trends – included: China, the Philippines, Korea, Taiwan, Vietnam, Laos, Cambodia, and Indonesia in East Asia; Israel, Saudi Arabia, Iran, and Egypt in the Middle East; Congo in Africa; Guatemala, Cuba, Nicaragua, and other small countries in Central America; and Brazil and Chile in Latin America. The motives and mechanisms of some of these interventions were discussed earlier. Here all that needs to be carried out is to underline some typical economic and political patterns that emerged under American tutelage. In such important cases as Vietnam, American intervention failed; this case does not need to be included in the present discussion of the impact of America's informal empire, except to note that the failed effort to establish such an empire destroyed that country's economy and led to the death of nearly three million Vietnamese. I will comment here instead on three other cases, namely, Iran, Chile, and South Korea; Iran and Chile help flesh out the typical impact, whereas the Korean exception needs to be explained.

In a country like Iran, the overthrow of Mossadegh not only forestalled the economic nationalization of oil but also cut short a promising move toward democracy. Recall a simple fact: Mossadegh had been elected. That the British and the Americans were threatened by his nationalist economic policies is understandable; the economic stakes were high. But overthrowing him via a covert coup and then supporting a pro-American dictator – the Shah of Iran – also destroyed the prospects of the emergence of a more tolerant political order in Iran. Over time, the Shah became increasingly dictatorial. He used the rhetoric of the Cold War to repress those within Iran who would have favored a more liberal political order. This drove opposition to the Shah and to his sponsor, the USA, underground. In a deeply religious country, it was difficult for the Shah to eliminate clerics as a potential political force. Over time, it was the ayatollahs – Shia clerics – who helped focus opposition to Shah into a revolution that overthrew the Shah in 1979. This finally ended the Anglo-American informal empire in Iran. However, the intolerant ayatollahs hardly provided a decent political alternative. The long-term political consequences of American intervention in Iran are thus still unfolding.

Meanwhile, to return to a discussion of the Shah's economic policies, the Shah gave back the control of Iranian oil to British and American companies, while sharing the profits. For the next quarter of a century, the Iranian economy was mainly an oil-exporting economy; rates of economic growth correlated highly with oil revenues. The Americans bought Iranian oil and the Shah used oil revenues to buy American arms. This served American interests in two ways: It helped bring back some of Iran's oil money to the USA; but, even more importantly, the Shah was an American proxy in the oil-rich Gulf, saving Americans heavy military expenditures in the region. Beyond this core contract – oil as a commodity in exchange for American-manufactured armaments – the Shah enjoyed some policy autonomy, both because this was the postcolonial twentieth century and because Iran bordered the Soviet Union. The Shah used this autonomy to pursue economic development at home, including some land redistribution and manufacturing; land reforms, however, were not all that successful and manufacturing only contributed some 10 percent of the GDP when the Shah lost power to the clerics. But still, the Iranian economy during the Shah's reign grew handsomely. This outcome is consistent with the main proposition being developed here, namely, client states within the purview of informal empire may experience commodity-led economic growth, but the weight of such arrangements is tilted against both nationalist and democratic politics, as well as against a more diversified economy.

Some two decades later, the USA again intervened in Chile to overthrow an elected socialist government. The impact on Chile was broadly similar to that on Iran. A major calamity of American intervention in Chile was of course that country's functioning democracy. Unlike Iran, Chile had practiced democracy for several decades. Over these decades, a variety of left-leaning forces had given voice to those at the bottom in a highly unequal society. Why this threatened the USA was discussed earlier. A segment of the Chilean elite then collaborated with the Americans to overthrow the socialist president, Allende. What followed was nearly two decades of dictatorial rule by the pro-American Pinochet. Pinochet's rule was ruthless and repressive. The scale of human rights violations of that regime are well documented (Kornbluh, 2004). Unlike Iran, however, Chile's democratic tradition had deeper roots. When the opposition to Pinochet grew, popular demands in Chile – and more broadly in the world – were for restoration of democracy and not for a theocracy. That democracy was returned to Chile was no thanks to the USA.

Economically, Pinochet compensated American companies handsomely. Many of these companies returned to Chile with yet newer investments. Land reforms were reversed. With the help of American economic advisors, Pinochet then set out to create a free-market model of development in Chile. The stakes were high for the USA too; this is because an important motive behind the coup was to discourage a drift toward social-democracy in Latin America. The USA thus whole heartedly supported Chile as a neoliberal poster child, including significant financial help. Under Pinochet, the Chilean economy grew at around 4 percent per annum; this was certainly better than many other Latin American economies. As noted earlier, Chile served as a model of sorts for the Washington Consensus, a country that avoided the more common pattern of low growth under conditions of informal empire. However, much of Chilean development under American tutelage was lop-sided. Wealth and income inequalities increased. The pattern of growth was the most telling indicator of impact of informal empire. Following the coup, international development organizations like the World Bank and others freely lent money to Chile, enabling it to pay back its foreign debtors, including many American banks. Chile also opened up its economy to foreign investors. They in turn produced goods mainly for domestic consumption. Chile continued to export commodities in exchange for manufactured goods. For example, Chile's manufactured exports as a percentage of total exports averaged some 15 percent toward the end of the Pinochet period; this compares with nearly 80 percent manufactured exports for countries like Malaysia and Thailand. Growth notwithstanding, the Chilean economy under a pro-American regime became more unequal and remained commodity-dependent.

The suggestion that America's informal empire mainly promoted lop-sided development may be met with an objection that cases like South Korea, Taiwan, and Israel do not really fit. This is because, in such cases, diversified economic development and a client status went hand in hand. While each of these cases requires a somewhat case-specific discussion, what they do have in common is that they served strong American strategic interests; instead of taking economic advantage of these countries, the USA sought to support them against external threats. A few comments on the case of South Korea may help clarify some underlying issues. The first thing to note is that the USA really did not intervene in South Korea. The USA inherited South Korea as a result of the Japanese defeat in World War II. In this important sense, the South Korean case is similar to West Germany, or even Japan, in that these countries became American client states as a result of World War II. The parallels between West Germany and South Korea are even stronger in the sense that both were seriously threatened by communism. The USA was then willing to put a lot of resources into strengthening these partial nation-states as part of defending the "free world."

American resource commitment, however, is far from sufficient to explain South Korea's eventual economic success. If it was, a country like South Vietnam ought to have survived and flourished. The heyday of American economic influence over South Korea was the presidency of Syngman Rhee. During that period (1948–1960), the South Korean economy hardly flourished. US foreign aid helped rebuild Japanese-created industries in South Korea. Other than that, neither the USA nor Rhee prioritized economic development. The results bore witness to alternate priorities, such as dealing with the communist threat. Rapid industrialization of South Korea only began under the presidency of Park Chung Hee (1963–1979). As is well known, Park hardly followed American economic advice to prosperity. Instead, he built on Korea's Japanese legacy, strengthened the inherited developmental state, partnered with big business, repressed labor, and used economic nationalism to facilitate rapid industrialization. Park then pursued state-supported export promotion as well as import substitution. Building on the Japanese model, South Korea succeeded heroically in creating a modern industrial economy. From the standpoint of the present study, the question that arises is: How did Park Chung Hee create policy autonomy within the frame of considerable dependency on the USA? And the answer is that in a client state where American interests were primarily strategic, the USA turned a blind eye to how such states pursued economic development. South Korea's rapid economic success actually helped strengthen South Korea's capacity to defend itself and thus helped America's core interests in the region. Understood as such, cases like South Korea are really not exceptions to the logic of America's informal empire; instead, they follow a different logic because America's interest in such cases was more strategic than economic.

4.3 Breaking the Shackles, or Not

Following the end of the Cold War, American interventions in the developing world did not come to an end. These more recent interventions have followed one of two pathways: soft imperialism, exemplified by the imposition of the Washington Consensus, especially on Latin America toward the end of the century; and hard imperialism, exemplified by the military intervention in Iraq in the new millennium. Once again, the motives and methods of such interventions were discussed earlier. The issue now is to note the impact of such continuing interventions. First, the impact of soft imperialism. This is best demonstrated by juxtaposing the economic performance of Latin America against that of Asia during the heyday of the Washington Consensus – say, 1980–2005. In general, important Asian countries performed much better on both growth and distribution dimensions during these years than Latin American countries. While the determinants of these different regional patterns are complex, an important underlying factor was that Latin American countries remained a lot more vulnerable to American pressure to embrace the Washington Consensus than Asian countries; post–World War II decolonization has been a lot more real in Asia than in Latin America, with long-term consequences.

Between 1980 and 2005, Latin American and Asian economies grew at 2.5 and 5.9 percent per annum, respectively.[22] The gap between the rich and poor in Latin America was also much wider than in Asia; the ratio of earnings of the top and bottom 20 percent in Latin America was nearly 1:20, while in Asia, it was 1:7. To repeat, why Asian countries performed much better than Latin American countries can not be fully answered in this Element. Nevertheless, the differing patterns of how the two regions came to be linked to the global economy were striking. The USA successfully pressured Latin American countries to open their economies, shrink their states, and embrace a more free-market model of development. Latin American countries also continued to depend more heavily on foreign resources for their economic growth. This dependent model of development contrasted with the more nationalist model of development pursued in many Asian countries. Nationalist states steered economic development in much of Asia, often relying on national economic resources. When Asian countries did depend on foreign investment, they tended to limit this dependence by encouraging firms from various countries to invest, as well as by decoupling technology from investment. Moreover, most Asian countries promoted exports of manufactured goods and controlled the movement of financial capital in and out of their countries. This nationalist model of development encouraged strategic rather than full integration with the world economy; it was this model, in turn, that was partially responsible for superior economic growth with modest inequalities in Asian countries. By contrast, the USA pushed Latin American countries to embrace a more open economy model under the rubric of Washington Consensus on development; this model, in turn, was again partially responsible for sluggish growth with sharp inequalities.

Why was the USA able to push Latin American countries to open their economies more so than Asian ones? The proximate reasons – I will return to the deeper reasons – had to do with the fact that Latin American countries were heavily indebted to American banks. For example, the debt service to export ratio for Latin America in 1980 was close to 40 percent, compared to 16 percent in much of Asia. This difference in turn was rooted in the fact that Latin American countries had borrowed more heavily during the 1970s than Asian countries, as well as in the fact that many Asian countries already exported

---

[22] Asian countries that are included in this calculation are: Bangladesh, China, India, Indonesia, Malaysia, Pakistan, the Philippines, South Korea, Taiwan, Thailand, and Vietnam. Latin American countries that are included are: Argentina, Bolivia, Brazil, Chile, Colombia, Ecuador, Mexico, Peru, and Venezuela.

larger shares of their GDP. With more foreign debt burden, Latin American countries needed access to foreign exchange during the 1980s so as to continue servicing their debt. Not only did this directly drain resources away from economic growth but leaders of Latin American countries had to approach the USA or US-dominated international organizations such as the World Bank or the IMF for loans. As discussed earlier, these external actors gave loans in exchange for policy reform, namely to embrace the open economy prescriptions rooted in the Washington Consensus. Many Asian countries were able to resist these pressures, though not all, and certainly not after the Asian financial crisis in the late 1990s.

Meanwhile, the deeper roots of the different developmental pathways of Asia versus Latin America at the end of the century lay in more or less sovereignty enjoyed by the two regions. Following World War II, many Asian countries finally broke the shackles of imperialism. For example, China had a communist revolution and India successfully pushed out the British via a mass nationalist movement. The Asian giants then prioritized state consolidation first and turned their focus sharply on economic development only in the 1980s. By contrast, most Latin American countries continued along grooves of earlier origin. So, again for example, Getúlio Vargas and Perón helped sustain significant continuities in the political economy of pre– and post–World War II Brazil and Argentina, respectively. Of course, Latin American countries also tried to pursue nationalist economic projects, such as import-substituting industrialization during the 1950s and the 1960s. However, they continued to depend on foreign investors to do so and focused on the production of consumer products for the domestic elite. Once this easy pathway to modernity ran out of steam, Latin American countries turned to foreign borrowing during the 1970s that, in turn, drove them to the debt crisis and into the arms of Washington again toward the end of the century. By contrast, with sovereign and consolidated states, Asian leaders used state intervention to create dynamic economies. China and India, for example, produced heavy industries at home and promoted manufactured exports abroad. In addition to the differing rates of economic growth and patterns of inequality that were noted earlier, another telling difference was this: By 2005, nearly 70 percent of total exports of Asian countries were manufactured goods, while those of Latin American ones were commodities. Clearly, the USA took advantage of the debt crisis faced by Latin American countries during the 1980s, forcibly opened their economies, and over the next quarter of a century, the economies of the region experienced sluggish growth with high income inequalities, and remained commodity exporters.

The impact of America's hard militarism on Iraq is still unfolding. While most American troops have left Iraq by now, no one doubts that, if needed, they

can return. Meanwhile, the two most important legacies of American intervention in Iraq are: a nearly failed state; and denationalization of Iraqi oil. As noted
earlier, once Americans had occupied Iraq, they dismantled the old Baathist
state. The old state under Saddam Hussein, odious as it was, still provided
a semblance of order and security for most Iraqis. Once this was dismantled,
a variety of hostilities in society, some latent, others new, came to the surface.
Violence came to grip much of Iraq under American occupation. Even a large
American troop presence failed to provide order. Worse, Americans imagined
a new Iraqi state as composed mainly of ethnic groups: Shias, Sunnis, and
Kurds. This fed ethnic hostilities that, over time, became virulent. Shias and
Sunnis attacked each other's holy sites and Kurds sought increasing autonomy.
Iraqi nationalists wanted the USA out and neighboring states like Iran fished in
troubled waters, supporting one militia against another. Nearly half a million
Iraqis died during American occupation. After the American troops left in 2011,
truly extreme groups like ISIS took advantage of the authority vacuum and
entered the fray. American troops then returned to Iraq to deal with ISIS. The
efforts to form a stable democratic government since then have often proved
elusive. Governance in American-shaped Iraq continues to be plagued by
instability, corruption, poor management of the economy, and a failure to
deliver public services.

Oil is central to Iraq's economy and, as discussed earlier, was also crucial in
American calculations to undertake an expensive military intervention. While
much of the Iraqi state and economy was destroyed during American occupation, enormous effort went into preserving the extraction and export of Iraqi oil.
Any one who doubts that oil was an important motive behind American
intervention needs to explain why only this one sector of the economy was
protected during the American occupation. As important, Iraq's state-owned oil
company was privatized under American tutelage. A number of major foreign
private oil companies – Western and non-Western – now operate Iraqi oil fields.
While the Iraqi state shares the resulting profits, so do foreign companies;
ownership and control are also now fragmented, weakening the Iraqi state.
The Iraqi economy continues to be heavily dependent on oil exports and
revenues. Iraq's GDP fluctuates with oil earnings, and export earnings are
nearly all oil earnings. Manufacturing contributes only a miniscule share of
Iraq's national production. For the near future, Iraq is likely to continue to be
a poorly functioning state, with sprinkles of oil riches here and there.

In sum, leaving aside American rhetoric of bringing democracy and free-
market–led prosperity to the developing world, the regions of the word under
significant American influence have not fared well. Latin America and the
Middle East are two such regions in which the USA has undertaken significant

interventions in the post–Cold War period. The USA used its enhanced leverage during the debt crisis to further open up Latin American economies. The impact on Latin America was mostly negative. This is not only a scholarly judgment. A significant portion of citizens of Latin American countries share this view. At the time of this writing (December 2021), for example, Chile has again elected a leftist leader, committed to reversing the legacy of American-supported neoliberalism. Will the USA support such a shift, or at least quietly step aside, respecting democratic verdicts? The past does not offer reasons for optimism. In the Middle East too, US troops have withdrawn from Afghanistan, leaving Afghans at the mercy of the Taliban. It is telling that, by contrast, the US withdrawal from oil-rich Iraq is considerably more partial. Sadly, the impact of US influence over Iraq has hardly brought good government or a diversified economy to that country. Only time will tell if Iraqis on their own are able to carve out a functioning state that, in turn, might put the enormous natural wealth of that country to good use. Meanwhile, it is important to note that imperialism has hardly vanished in the twenty-first century: With their own prosperity and power in mind, metropolitan states continue to intervene when possible, hurting the life chances of those living in the poorer parts of the world.

5 Conclusion

Greed moves imperialism and guns make it possible. Imperial subjugation in turn hurts the prospects of creating prosperous societies in the global periphery. The rich and the powerful then cover up their base behavior by either focusing on the few good things that they did transmit to peripheral countries via imperial rule, or by simply denying that their actions add up to imperialism. Some scholars also help provide a fig leaf for imperial powers by suggesting that imperial actions are driven more by security and less by economic concerns. It is as if actions in self-defense will be judged less morally reprehensible than premeditated acts of self-aggrandizement. The evidence reviewed in this Element suggests instead that imperialism was often moved by the metropolitan urge to enhance national prosperity. The main method to achieve imperial ambitions was to limit the sovereignty of peripheral countries. This tactic ensured that peripheral economies remained open and accessible to imperial powers. Loss of sovereignty, however, severely restricted the scope for constructive political action and deliberate economic development in peripheral countries. The main proposition of this Element then is that sovereignty is an economic asset in the modern world; it is a precondition for the emergence of states that can foster prosperous and inclusive economies.

To move toward a conclusion, all that needs to be done is to tease out some implications of this argument and to speculate about the near-future trends. As to practical implications of the argument developed in this study, metropolitan countries need to come to terms with their imperial past. This past contributed to their economic well-being at the expense of poor countries of the world. Recognition of this fact may not come easily. However, it is morally the right thing to do. As important, if countries like Britain and the USA hope to be viewed as models of liberalism to the world, liberal hypocrisy on imperialism remains a major hurdle. For example, when Western countries preach liberalism to China, the Chinese can readily point to the nineteenth century of humiliation, when Britain forcibly opened up China for selling opium, all in the name of liberal free trade. When the USA champions self-determination for nations, many in the developing world wonder why the USA fought such nationalists as Ho Chi Minh? When the USA wants to be seen as a beacon of democracy, some in the developing world see a different USA, a USA that helped overthrow democratically elected leaders in countries as diverse as Iran, Guatemala, Congo, and Chile. And when the USA peddles advice on how to run prosperous economies, some in the developing world again see a design to benefit American corporations in cahoots with their elites. It is difficult to occupy a high moral ground or to exercise soft power in the world with such hypocrisy writ large.

For developing countries, the main implication of this study can be stated as a parable: Beware of the powerful when they come offering help. The history of imperialism is a history of the rich and the powerful taking advantage of the poor in the name of doing good. This pattern is likely to continue. In the end, if the developing countries wish to avoid imperial traps, they will have to help themselves. The task of creating more livable societies in the twenty-first century will remain a self-help project. And for such a project to progress, what will be needed is leadership from sovereign and effective nation-states. There is no other way around it. No sizable country has ever developed under foreign tutelage. Where sovereignty is limited, the challenge is how to loosen the constraints. Where sovereign states remain ineffective, the challenge is how to construct better states. Where sovereign and effective states exist, progress is underway.

Finally, what about the near-future trends, especially the continuing role of the USA and the emerging role of China? Is the USA likely to continue to intervene in countries where it believes its economic interests are at stake? While the whims of leaders are impossible to predict, structural conditions do point to some possible trends. Enormous power inequality between the USA and most developing countries of the world readily creates the temptation for the USA to intervene when opportunities to enhance its interests become available. However, superior military power is not always sufficient to translate ambitions into favorable outcomes; the USA can readily win wars but often fails at creating stable-but-subservient states. Nationalism and mobilized masses in peripheral countries remain a formidable obstacle. It is thus not surprising that many US interventions – power advantage notwithstanding – have failed to achieve their goals. The failure in Vietnam gave a pause to American interventions. The triumphalism at the end of the Cold War put an end to these hesitations. Again, however, the US intervention in Afghanistan was an expensive failure, and the results of the war in Iraq are also hardly unambiguous. Closer to home too, the USA failed to get rid of Nicolás Maduro in Venezuela. Will such failures deter the USA in the near future? They should, but they probably won't. Wants are insatiable and power creates arrogance. So, for example, if the new leftist leader in Chile comes to be viewed as a threat, some members of Washington's political class will surely argue that the ambitions of such upstarts in America's backyard must be thwarted.

Is China likely to be a new imperial power? While it is too early to tell, some trends are evident. There are strong parallels between cases of historical economic expansion discussed in this Element and China's more recent search for economic opportunities abroad (Brautigam, 2009; Jenkins, 2018; Stallings, 2020). Rapid economic growth at home has generated pressures in China to expand overseas. On the trade front, for example, as in the case of Britain and the USA in the past, China now exports mainly manufactured goods and imports giant amount of raw materials. China's trade relations with Africa and Latin America thus clearly follow a colonial or neocolonial pattern. China's foreign investment has also grown, often spear-headed by state-owned firms in search of such natural resources as oil and minerals. And China's huge foreign reserves allow it to lend money for projects that, in turn, facilitate Chinese exports of higher-value-added goods. Unpaid debts also create dependency, underlining again the strong role of finance in modern imperialism. China's economic expansion abroad then is broadly in line with a central proposition of this Element, namely, that the pursuit of national economic prosperity generates a tendency toward overseas economic expansion.

The impact of China's economic expansion is also generally similar to patterns noted earlier in cases of informal empire. Integration with the Chinese economy has facilitated commodity-led growth in some developing countries but has inhibited industrialization. The underlying mechanisms are not hard to understand. Growing Chinese demand for specific commodities – such as soya beans or iron ore – helps those developing countries that are in a position to export these products to China. China's overall demand for commodities also fuels higher global prices. Higher volumes and prices of commodities have fed higher rates of economic growth in some African and Latin American countries. This impact is especially notable when Chinese economic growth – and thus China's demand – has decelerated, causing decline in economic growth in commodity-exporting economies. Chinese loans and foreign investments may also help economic growth in some such countries as Pakistan but are not large enough to make a noticeable impact on such other economies like Nigeria or Brazil. Still, infrastructure loans are welcomed by many developing (and even some developed) economies. Conversely, the fear of falling into debt traps is also growing. More important, China's cheap manufactured goods have undercut the prospects of industrial development, especially in African countries. Even in middle-income Latin American countries, there is some evidence to suggest that China's economic expansion is causing deindustrialization (Stallings, 2020). One underlying mechanism is suggested, say, by the impact on Mexico: Sale of cheaper Chinese manufactured goods in the USA have undercut the prospects of new industries in Mexico that were hoping to succeed by exporting to the USA. In broad terms then, China's economic expansion is perpetuating a pattern of global division of labor between those who sell commodities and those who produce higher-value-added manufactured goods.

Where China's economic expansion differs from Anglo-American imperialism of the past is in the limited use of military intervention, at least so far. China did not need to send gunboats anywhere to open economies. For better or worse, China just stepped into the open economy imperium created by the USA during the heyday of the Washington Consensus. With a competitive economy, China then came to dominate the global market for manufactured exports; voracious need for commodities, in turn, helped create complementarities between the Chinese economy on the one side and African and Latin American economies on the other side.[23] In the aftermath of two decades of Washington-sponsored structural adjustment programs in the late twentieth century, many developing countries also welcomed unconditional Chinese foreign investments and loans in the new millennium. None of this means that China's economic interactions with the developing world are largely benign; on the contrary, they are increasingly beginning to resemble the more classic cases of informal empire, especially those cases where the main instrument of coercion was economic. Several examples point in this direction: Reports have emerged that Chinese firms have bribed officials in African countries to secure favorable contracts, as well as interfered in

---

[23] I do not include other Asian economies here because China's economic relations, say, with Southeast Asian countries is a lot more complex than the exchange of manufactured goods for commodities.

elections here and there; unpaid loans have led to the Chinese acquiring an important port in Sri Lanka; a country like Pakistan is now heavily dependent on Chinese support; newly elected officials in Malaysia demanded a new contract on better terms from China, and succeeded, only to underline that the Chinese are more than willing to take advantage of poorly governed countries; and economic choices of many countries in Africa are narrowing as they become indebted to China. So, China is very much moving toward establishing its own informal empire. Nevertheless, it bears repeating that China's economic expansion has so far proceeded without overt use of military force. This may change. Also, Chinese hesitation to use force more likely reflects their relative global power position rather than any higher commitment to nonintervention.

To conclude, overseas imperialism of great powers has a long and pernicious history. In this Element I have underlined some recurring patterns evident in this long history. First, there is the issue of why imperialists imperialize. Clearly, no simple answer can help explain the enormous complexity that historical evidence presents. And yet, the preponderance of evidence suggests that a key driver of imperialism is the urge of powerful states to enhance the economic prosperity of their respective countries. Second, the main method of imperialism is to undermine sovereignty in the global periphery. In order to have ready economic access to poor countries, what imperialists need are stable-but-subservient regimes in power. Depending on circumstances, both formal and informal empire have facilitated such access. And finally, there is the most important issue of the impact of colonialism. Again, enormous variations notwithstanding, the evidence suggests that there is an inverse relationship between imperialism and development. Formal colonies hardly experienced any growth or industrialization. Some growth took place in countries that were controlled informally, but that growth tended to be lop-sided: very little industrialization and skewed benefits. Bu contrast, the rare and successful cases of inclusive development in the twenty-first century underline the importance of sovereign and effective states.

References

Abrahamian, Ervand (2013). *The Coup: 1953, the CIA, and the Roots of Modern U.S.–Iranian Relations*. New York: New Press.

Bacevich, Andrew J. (2016). *America's War for the Greater Middle East: A Military History*. New York: Random House.

Bhagwati, Jagdish (2004). *In Defense of Globalization*. New York: Oxford University Press.

Brautigam, Deborah (2009). *The Dragon's Gift: The Real Story of China in Africa*. New York: Oxford University Press.

Broadberry, Stephen, Johan Custodis, and Bishnupriya Gupta (2015). "India and the Great Divergence: An Anglo-Indian Comparison of Per Capita GDP, 1600–1871," *Explorations in Economic History*, 55, 58–75.

Burbank, Jane, and Fredrick Cooper (2010). *Empires in World History*. Princeton, NJ: Princeton University Press.

Cain, P. J., and Anthony Hopkins (2002). *British Imperialism, 1688–2000*. New York: Longman.

Cohen, Benjamin (1973). *The Question of Imperialism: The Political Economy of Dominance and Dependence*. New York: Basic Books.

Darwin, John (2009). *The Empire Project*. New York: Cambridge University Press.

Duus, Peter (1984). "Economic Dimensions of Meiji Imperialism: The Case of Korea, 1895–1910," in Ramon H. Myers and Mark R. Peattie, eds., *The Japanese Colonial Empire, 1895–1945*, 128–170. Princeton, NJ: Princeton University Press.

Eisenstadt, Shmuel N. (1993). *The Political System of Empires*. New York: Routledge.

Ferguson, Niall (2003). *The Rise and Demise of British World Order and Lessons for Global Power*. New York: Basic Books.

Gaddis, John Lewis (1997). *Now We Know: Rethinking Cold War History*. Oxford: Clarendon Press.

Gallagher, John, and Ronald Robinson (1953). "The Imperialism of Free Trade," *Economic History Review*, Second Series, 6, no. 1, 1–15.

Graham, Richard (1969). "Sepoys and Imperialists: Techniques of British Power in Nineteenth-Century Brazil," *Inter-American Economic Affairs*, 23, 23–37.

Grandin, Greg (2000). *The Blood of Guatemala: A History of Race and Nation*. Durham, NC: Duke University Press.

Healy, David (1988). *Drive to Hegemony: The United States in the Caribbean, 1898–1917.* Madison: University of Wisconsin Press.

Hobsbawm, Eric (1989). *The Age of Empire, 1875–1914.* New York: Vintage Books.

Hobson, J. A. (1902). *Imperialism: A Study.* New York: James Pott and Company.

Hyam, Ronald (1976). *Britain's Imperial Century, 1815–1914.* London: B. T. Batsford.

Issawi, Charles (1961). "Egypt since 1800: A Study in Lop-sided Development," *The Journal of Economic History*, 21, no. 1, 1–25.

Jenkins, Rhys (2018). *How China Is Reshaping the Global Economy: Development Impact in Africa and Latin America.* New York: Oxford University Press.

Kohli, Atul (2004). *State-Directed Development: Political Power and Industrialization in the Global Periphery.* New York: Cambridge University Press.

Kohli, Atul (2020). *Imperialism and the Developing World: How Britain and the United States Shaped the Global Periphery.* New York: Oxford University Press.

Kornbluh, Peter (2004). *The Pinochet File: A Declassified Dossier of Atrocity and Accountability.* New York: New Press.

LaFeber, Walter (1993). *The American Search for Opportunity, 1865–1913.* New York: Cambridge University Press.

Leffler, Melvyn P. (1992). *A Preponderance of Power: National Security, the Truman Administration, and the Cold War.* Stanford, CA: Stanford University Press.

Llorca-Jaña, Manuel (2012). *The British Textile Trade in South America in the Nineteenth Century.* New York: Cambridge University Press.

Madison, Angus (2007). *Contours of the World Economy, 1–2030 AD.* New York: Oxford University Press.

Mamdani, Mahmood (1996). *Citizen and Subject: Contemporary Africa and the Legacy of Late Colonialism.* Princeton, NJ: Princeton University Press.

McCormick, Thomas J. (1967). *China Market: America's Quest for Informal Empire, 1893–1901.* Chicago: Quadrangle Books.

Osterhammel, Jürgen (1999). "Britain and China, 1842–1914," in Andrew Porter, ed., *Oxford History of the British Empire: The Nineteenth Century*, vol. 3, 146–169. Oxford: Oxford University Press.

Palma, Gabriel (1978). "Dependency: A Formal Theory of Underdevelopment or a Methodology for the Analysis of Concrete Situations of Underdevelopment?" *World Development*, 6, nos. 7–8, 881–924.

Schumpeter, Joseph (1951). *Imperialism and Social Classes*. Translated by Heinz Norden. New York: A. M. Kelly. Original German edition published in 1919.

Stallings, Barbara (2020). *Dependency in the Twenty First Century? The Political Economy of China–Latin American Relations*. New York: Cambridge University Press.

Stiglitz, Joseph (2003). *Globalization and Its Discontents*. New York: W. W. Norton.

Wallerstein, Immanuel (1974). "The Rise and Future Demise of the Capitalist World System: Concepts for Comparative Analysis," *Comparative Studies in Society and History*, 16, no. 4, 387–415.

Williams, William Appleman (1962). *The Tragedy of American Diplomacy*. New York: Dell.

Young, Marilyn B. (1991). *The Vietnam Wars, 1945–1990*. New York: Harper Collins.

Acknowledgments

The comments of Stephan Haggard and of another anonymous reviewer were helpful in revising this manuscript.

Cambridge Elements ☰

Politics of Development

Rachel Beatty Riedl
Einaudi Center for International Studies and Cornell University

Rachel Beatty Riedl is the Director and John S. Knight Professor of the Einaudi Center for International Studies and Professor in the Government Department and School of Public Policy at Cornell University. Riedl is the author of the award-winning *Authoritarian Origins of Democratic Party Systems in Africa* (2014) and co-author of *From Pews to Politics: Religious Sermons and Political Participation in Africa* (with Gwyneth McClendon, 2019). She studies democracy and institutions, governance, authoritarian regime legacies, and religion and politics in Africa. A former Kellogg Institute visiting fellow at the University of Notre Dame, Yale Program on Democracy Fellow, Faculty Fulbright Scholar, Chair of the APSA section Democracy and Autocracy, and Fellow and Director of the Scientific Council at the Institute for Advanced Study (Nantes), she holds a PhD from Princeton University. Riedl was a term member of the Council on Foreign Relations and has conducted policy analysis on issues pertaining to governance, elections, democratic representation and identity politics. She serves on the Editorial Committee of World Politics and the Editorial Board of African Affairs, Comparative Political Studies, Journal of Democracy, and Africa Spectrum. She is co-host of the podcast Ufahamu Africa.

Ben Ross Schneider
Massachusetts Institute of Technology

Ben Ross Schneider is Ford International Professor of Political Science at MIT and Director of the MIT-Brazil program. Prior to moving to MIT in 2008, he taught at Princeton University and Northwestern University. His books include *Business Politics and the State in 20th Century Latin America* (2004), *Hierarchical Capitalism in Latin America* (2013), *Designing Industrial Policy in Latin America: Business-Government Relations and the New Developmentalism* (2015), and *New Order and Progress: Democracy and Development in Brazil* (2016). He has also written on topics such as economic reform, democratization, education, labor markets, inequality, and business groups.

Advisory Board

About the Series

The Element series *Politics of Development* provides important contributions on
`both established and new topics on the politics and political economy of developing
countries. A particular priority is to give increased visibility to a dynamic and growing
body of social science research that examines the political and social determinants of
economic development, as well as the effects of different development models on
political and social outcomes.

Mario Einaudi

CENTER FOR
INTERNATIONAL STUDIES

Cambridge Elements $\equiv$

Politics of Development

Elements in the Series

Developmental States
Stephan Haggard

Coercive Distribution
Michael Albertus, Sofia Fenner and Dan Slater

Participation in Social Policy: Public Health in Comparative Perspective
Tulia G. Falleti and Santiago L. Cunial

Undocumented Nationals: Between Statelessness and Citizenship
Wendy Hunter

Democracy and Population Health
James W. McGuire

Rethinking the Resource Curse
Benjamin Smith and David Waldner

Greed and Guns: Imperial Origins of the Developing World
Atul Kohli

A full series listing is available at: www.cambridge.org/EPOD

Printed in the United States
by Baker & Taylor Publisher Services